Acknowledgments

Consider this a memoir, a collection of all my thoughts, ideas, and experiences I've lived as an indie author since I began this journey. It took about two years to gather up and organize all my writings kept in notebooks, journals, on scraps of paper, napkins and old Word files, which have been put into this book. Some sections may repeat the same thoughts and message, but they stand alone unedited for they were written at different times in my life.

This is meant to be a raw piece of work I feel fit to be put out there as a means to move forward as an indie author and to show and inspire any aspiring writer who reads this. For those who have no ambitions of becoming an indie author, I hope that you are able to find and take some gems from this book which you can utilize with your life and whatever dreams you chase or with what you are passionate about.

The beauty of being human is having the dreams that we possess and the journeys that we take. Every person on this Earth is their own, everyone is unique, and although many lives run parallel, some in opposite directions, no matter what path you are on, you are your own entity who is capable of turning your dreams into reality, and manifesting the path that you want to take. It all starts from within, as with the desire to become an independent author.

The indie author's path isn't easy, nor is it one many aspiring writers are willing to travel or take to the end. For me it has been a growing experience and rewarding. This I will share with you and give you some insight as to the state of mind I was in, what the writing process and journey was like and what it took for me to take a seed of an idea from the time I decided I wanted to take this indie author's path to manifesting all that I've learned and created into a published book.

An Indie Author's Way

By:

Tommy Tutalo

Part I
A Blind Leap

Great Expectations

What you will find within this book is a piece of me. You will learn about who I am, where I came from, the 10 year journey I took writing my first novel Esperanza, and the life I lived as an indie author.

My goal is to not only share with you my life and journey but also to guide aspiring writers with my words. I hope to somehow inspire you to chase your dreams no matter how big or how small.

The unconventional ways in which I lived may not be in tuned with the so called norm of society nor the right way to live life. In the eyes of the blind I was considered a fool, but a fool foolishly dancing his way through life. Those who couldn't hear the music I heard never knew the symphony playing in my head and the passion beating in my heart.

The dreams in which I chased were never understood nor were they considered of any worth. My dreams and myself were something to laugh at and mock. I was the subject of ridicule, an easy target to say negative things about from simple minded people, from those in my life, from those who I crossed paths with, from those who I worked with, even from those with smiles, from those I walked with and from those who were supposed to love me.

To be humiliated is part of being human, it is what we learn from and grow from spiritually as we partake on this journey called life. It in a way is a blessing in disguise, a necessity in order to become stronger from within and carry on. The greatest fear in life is the fear of worrying about what others think. Once you are able to overcome this fear the road is smoother, life flows easier, and you'll write without holding back your deepest thoughts and desires.

Writing is a gift that all have but not many are willing to nurture, transform into their own and manifest a book or a story told. In this book you will find what to expect if you choose to venture down the writer's path.

This isn't a step by step guide nor is this a how to, or a "writing for dummies" type of book. Inside this book you will find the process which worked for me, all that I learned, the elements and thoughts that helped me and guided me along my way. The journey has transformed me in so many ways and I hope that this book and my words are able to transform you in some way for the better.

Words are powerful, my goal is to have my words bring you inspiration, trigger a positive emotional drive deep within your heart, bring you mental and spiritual growth, and motivate you to take the leap down the indie author's path as did I.

About

So who's Tommy? I'm an independent author, writer, photographer, painter, and visual artist, whose work is considered to be diverse, and universal. A native of West Orange, New Jersey, I come from a hardworking, and loving blue-collar background, and grew up in an ethnically diverse community. Both my up-bringing and the melting pot I grew up in have been two influential factors in my life and the arts. At an early age I discovered a love for both the arts and the beautiful game, soccer. Soccer would become my outlet and craft, which I would nourish and pursue, putting the arts off as secondary. My hard work ethic, devotion, and perseverance with soccer, would enable me to play at a very high level during my adolescent years, becoming one of the most decorated and recognized players in New Jersey, and eventually sought by, and play for The Richard Stockton College of New Jersey, where I would win a DIV. III National Championship with the 2001 team. This would be the pinnacle of my soccer career, and the foundation for the next phase in my life. As one door shut, another door opened, and I would then pursue the arts, learning many different art mediums during, and after graduating from college, with a Bachelor of the Arts degree, Art History, and by any means devote my life to living as an independent artist and author.

Here I am now. It's November 14, 2018, the tail end of autumn. As I write this, my first novel Esperanza has been published for a little more than a year. Sales have been very modest and I have been spending the past year building up my personal brand, social media brand, networking, getting reviews, marketing, and working on the edits and rewrites for my second novel The Mime and other side projects such as this book.

What I am writing now is a book project I have been putting together since I published Esperanza. During and after the 10 years I spent writing it, I have accumulated pages of notes, and thoughts regarding the process, the story, and the state of mind I was in. Currently as I transition from my "break from writing" period of the year, September to early November, I am using this as a warm up to get back into a rhythm before I go full throttle again with The Mime. This I feel is the perfect project because during the past two and a half months of down time I have put together all of the notes, thoughts and newly added material to form this book. Along with the help of my brother Joey Tutalo, a master graphic designer who will help with creating the book cover, I hope to make something unique; a stimulating book that gives some in sight as to who I am, my journey writing my first novel, and what worked for me, and share my ideas, thoughts, and philosophies on the craft of writing. Ultimately this is my take on an indie author's manifesto.

I'm a Pisces; an introvert, empathic fish out of water. My whole life I have been the shy and quiet one, the loner who kept to himself and never opened up emotionally to others or shared my deepest thoughts. As a child I would be mocked by other students and considered a fool by teachers. It all used to bother me and hold me back in life, being the way I was and not understanding why I never quite fitted in with the others, the "normal" ones. I was an alienated dreamer and I still am today, an alienated adult now still chasing dreams.

It was difficult growing up this way. My self-esteem was very low and the decisions I made were out of fear of what others would think. My heart wanted me to go one way but my lack of competence kept me away from the opportunities and doors which would have taken me to different places. Would I be who I am today or where I am if I wasn't so driven by fear? Maybe not, but the one thing I do know for a fact is that all of the negative people, words and actions which consumed me are what watered me and helped me grow into the wiser and stronger person that I now am, a dreamer not afraid to chase his dreams.

My consciousness has expanded and my heart has opened up as vast as the universe. The spiritual journey I was born into and took molded me into the person I now am, and the awakening process which has happened in stages has opened my mind and eyes wider than before. I was and still am called "crazy", "weird", "strange", "there's something wrong with him", but then again being considered crazy by those who are still sheep of the systematic servitude of living a "normal life", and victims of cultural conditioning is a compliment. But I am not crazy, I am awake in an insane society, for that exact reason most people will call me crazy, for I am not afraid to chase a dream many do not understand. For I walk alone as I travel down the indie author's path my way.

<u>Life</u>

<u>Life Path/Experiences/Philosophies/My Journey</u>

This life journey I took is no different than any others yet, each person walks their own path. Being a human being and having the conscious experience we all have on this frequency plane, here on Earth is a gift. Each waking day is a day to learn and grow until the full expansion of consciousness is obtained.

Writing for me has opened up so many doors both internally and externally, but before I was a writer or the artist that I am, I was first an athlete. Soccer was the stepping stone to get me to where I now am as an indie author.

Soccer came natural to me. I started playing when I was five years old and I still play today. Not only was soccer fun to play growing up, but as I became a young teenager it was my passion. It was all I thought about every single day, all day, and even in my sleep. I dreamt of being a professional soccer player and it was during the 1994 World Cup that I wanted to be as good of a player as Roberto Baggio. I wanted to play professional soccer when I got older. And so, the journey began.

I had no guidance or personal trainers. I taught myself how to play. All I did every single day was spend hours alone in my backyard juggling, dibbling, and kicking the ball around. I would watch professional games on T.V. which at the time the only weekly games being shown were the

Mexican league games and the Italian Serie A games. MLS had just started but it wasn't as enriching to watch. The Champions League started to be shown in the U.S as I became a high school student and the English Premier league as well. Mostly reruns of previously recorded games, but they were still fun to watch and learn from. There was no internet like there is today to watch a game from anywhere in the world or digital cable. No Youtube either.

The act of playing every day, watching games and emulating what the players were doing on the pitch is what made me the exceptional player that I was. There was no magic. It was all me. I was a pioneer, with an entrepreneurial spirit and work ethic without even knowing it. This entrepreneurial spirit and work ethic I have wired in me is what has helped me become the soccer player I became and the indie author that I am now.

In the beginning when I decided I wanted to write and pursue the life of a writer, it was difficult. I didn't know where to begin or how to pursue the path of a writer. It was like starting all over again with soccer. The way I was trying to juggle a soccer ball for the first time is the feeling and way I was with my writing. It was a struggle, and having no guidance or knowledge of the craft wasn't helpful. I basically dove head first into the deep end.

It was during my final two years of college that I decided I would pursue this path. I took a semester off from school after finishing my first four years and when soccer came to an end, I went through a depression state of being of not knowing what to do with my life. Soccer was all I knew and all I was good at and it ended. What I did know at the time was that I wanted to become an artist. I painted and did some photography at the time, but writing was the art form that I connected with and fell in love with. For me it was going to be the stepping stone to someday become a film maker which to me at this time is the highest art form.

It was the summer of 2004 when I began writing in a journal. I started out by writing short poems, songs, my thoughts and my feelings. The only writing background I had was from writing assignments from grade school, journalism classes I took in high school and a handful of creative writing courses I took in college. I used what I learned, and what I remembered as a means to my approach to writing. What I did have from soccer was a strong work ethic. I wrote as often as I would train for soccer. I was disciplined and created a writing schedule and made sure to devote each day to writing for a certain amount of time. For the next two years I filled notebooks, and journals. I began outlining stories and writing some short stories. Finally after graduating from college December 2006, I decided to write a book.

It was early 2007 when I was in pursuit of writing a book. First I needed a story. Out of all the short stories I wrote at the time the one that stuck with me and grew was a story about a struggling artist who ends up as a care taker for a young girl. This story eventually grew bigger and bigger. It was then after creating the character Gabriela an illegal immigrant from Mexico, who was the mother of the child that the foundation for Esperanza was created. The story evolved around these three characters, and it was June 2007 when I began to write Esperanza. By the end of summer, August 2007 I completed my first draft, a 300 page manuscript. The dream of becoming an indie author had officially begun, but little did I know it was going to take me 10 years to finally finish Esperanza and get it published. And so the journey began.

Esperanza
The 10 Year Journey/Process

I remember speaking with an indie author at the time I finished my first draft, who told me her first book took 13 years to complete and publish. The young foolish writer I was at the time thought that, that was a bit too long to write a book. Well, it wasn't too long for a first book nor was it an easy road. I now find myself quit often now as the indie author forewarning aspiring writers about the long journey that awaits them with writing their first book.

Even though everyone is different, writing different kinds of books, with different aspirations, the process is still the same. The process never changes. It may be approached differently or utilized to the liking of the individual writer but all writing journeys require the same kind of discipline. If there was one virtue or character trait to put on the pyramid of necessary traits needed to complete a book, discipline would be the stone cap at the very top.

Discipline is what got me through the 10 years. Without it I may not have ever finished Esperanza or it wouldn't have become what it is today. It takes a strong mind to overcome the many obstacles a writer faces. Some of the thresholds I've experienced were periods of writer's block, spending a lot of time writing scenes, chapters, pages only to go back and either omit them or completely change them.

This journey didn't begin with curiosity or the want to become the most famous writer in the world. It began with the yearning to live my life as a writer. I guess you could say that I have the soul of a writer, but there was something more burning within my heart and soul, the calling we all get when we discover our purpose. That's how I felt with writing and when I began to write Esperanza, but without discipline and the entrepreneurial spirit and methodology I possess I may not be where I am now.

It's the process which got me through the 10 years. The strict weekly writing schedule I created for myself, the goals I set and conquered day after day, being able to face failures, overcome them and carry on, finding balance with writing and life, keeping mentally and physically fit, learning every day from my mistakes, and growing every day from all I've learned and educated myself about the writing principles, which for me are guidelines. These are some of the elements of success which I utilized.

Even more challenging was the unknown path I chose to take. I never knew when I was going to finish or where the road would take me. All I knew was that I was on the right path and believed that it would take me there.

Finding my voice

I'm still searching for it. I haven't really discovered my true potential yet, and I feel that as a human being, as the saying goes we all wear different masks. So, it is necessary to use a different voice, with the many different masks that we wear throughout our lives. This is true as a writer.

The one thing I understood from the very beginning when I began to write was that I wasn't going to write just one genre, or write stories based on what is trendy or popular at the moment (Vampires, Zombies, Harry Potter fantasy stories, or some story about cats). As a writer I always saw myself as a storyteller, someone who tells many different stories. In order to do so, and be effective the voice needs to change, constantly. You need to be adaptable, and able to write drama, suspense, comedy, etc. There is no right or wrong way to do this, but you do need to change your voice in order to make this work, and in order to discover your own, you must keep writing until a seed is planted. Intertwined within all the different writing styles you produce are the elements from which your true voice will grow and rise.

This will take time so have patience. Some may never discover their writing voice, but don't allow this fear to ever hold you back. Write, and continue to write until people begin to listen and respond then will you know you have created a voice. Will this voice be the one that defines you? For some yes, but for others it may be a single serving identity or the phantom self we become trapped within.

A writer's voice is precious, it can have power and influence; like magic it can change people and the world. So be aware of this and know that no matter what others think, your voice has meaning. So don't let it die within you, and don't ever stop searching until it is found.

As I mentioned before I am still searching for my voice. Have I had a glimpse of what my writer's voice is? Yes. Do I know where it will take me, no, but that is the beauty of the journey and the writing process. Never knowing where the road will take you and what you may find. The writer's voice is the gold at the end of the rainbow and that which I am still seeking and will never stop until it's found or I die.

Work Ethic

Your approach to anything you choose to do in life is essential. Having a strong and grounded work ethic is a part of this. No matter what it is you do in life or with your life, a key element in being successful is how you work. There is a difference between being a work-a-holic and an efficient worker. Being a work-a-holic may seem as though you're being productive, but usually what ends up happening is you become more stressed, and can waste lots of time. You could put hours into a project and end up not finishing, or getting the results that you want. It's all about quality, work smarter not harder.

Time is also a factor in producing positive results. Yes, time is an essential part of having a strong work ethic, but more importantly it's all about balance and discipline.

For me it was setting a strict schedule, and time frame to write and work on my writing projects. Each day I would find a time slot for when I can write, and would use that time to write. This could be from writing for 2hrs, 4hrs, 6hrs, or sometimes 8hrs. It all depended on the mood, or state of mind I was in, which is also key. There were times when I could sit and write for 1 hour and get more writing and better quality writing done than sitting for 4-6hrs. But, no matter how long writing sessions were, or what time of the day I wrote, I made sure to stick with the schedule I created.

When I was single I had all the time in the world. I would usually write after my day job for 4-6hrs, and on weekends I would do two writing sessions on a Saturday. I would get up early write for about 4-6hrs, and then write again later in the day for another 2-4hrs. I look back at the beginning when I started writing Esperanza, and started working on other writing projects and averaged about 25-45hrs a week writing.

When I had a girlfriend, and then got married that time was cut in half. Yes, I have developed as a writer and was able to write more quickly with quality, but I had to change my schedule and routine. I had to balance my time between work, my girlfriend, and writing. With any type of change, at first it isn't easy, it's hard to accept, and takes time to adjust to. But I was able to, and with the support of my girlfriend, I was able to find and make the time to write.

When I had a daughter all the time I had left to write was gone. I was in the final stages of writing Esperanza, and was now sitting on multiple completed drafts of other writing projects. I was at an ending point, but still I needed that time to write, and edit. At first it was very frustrating, but once I was able to map out a new course and approach writing sessions were fitted into my daily life and productive. The beauty of finding a way to make it work was that it was a pleasure being able to balance quality time with my family and writing. I had to find time within a 24hr window that we have each day. What worked best for me at this point in my life was writing late at night and in the early hours of the day when my wife and daughter were sleeping. I was also able to write after work for an hour or two during this small window of free time I had. And this is what worked for me.

The work ethic that I had with my writing spawned from my days training as a soccer player. Knowing that I had to work on my craft every day in order to get better, knowing that I had to put in quality time, and stick with a strict work routine in order to surpass myself each day was crucial. And like anything in life, not every day is a walk in the park. I didn't create magic every time I wrote, or create a classical piece of literature. There were days when I sat for hours and stared at a blank sheet of paper with many different thoughts racing through my mind, or I scribbled a bunch of nonsense or lines on a piece of paper. Bad days come and go. It happens and you have to be able to not only accept it but be able to get past it, knowing that better days will come, and they do. There is nothing that can compare to having a great writing session. Being able to sit for hours without looking up as the world passes by, write easily 5 to 10 pages of great, quality work, and then by the time you're done you check the time to see that 4-6 hrs had past, when it only feels like an hour, is a magical moment for a writer.

Juggling multiple stories, outlines, and the realities of life

In order to make this work you need to have first developed a strong work ethic. As discussed in the previous section, being able to create a strict work schedule and sticking to it is essential in executing whatever project you are working on. Being able to balance and work on multiple projects all at once can seem overwhelming but in reality isn't, if you create and stick with a game plan.

You have to set small goals. With Esperanza, even though I had the big picture and the final result visualized, along the journey I set small goals to be completed. I would have a goal/end point I would want to reach each week. After reaching the goal I set for myself, if there were more days left in the week, or time during a writing session, the first thing I would do would be to map out the next goal, and then little by little begin to map out work on other projects.

Or sometimes what would happen is that on the bad writing days when I was unable to work on Esperanza, or write anything on it, I would focus my thoughts on another project. The beauty about working on other side projects, while focusing on the priority project, is that your approach isn't as strict. There really are no expectations. When you're in the development, early stages anything goes, there is no right or wrong way of writing. It's more fun.

One thing I've learned with writing is the closer you get to the end of a project the more stressful it can be. By the end point you have a finalized story which has rules and borders you need to stay within, regarding plot, characters and structure. At the beginning of any writing project nothing is really set in stone yet, so you can have fun, and enjoy the writing process more, because there is constant change happening. You don't have to worry about following a specific plot point, or sticking with a character's role. It's like molding wet clay into a pot.

There are then the times when the priority project will end up in the hands of the editor. This is a perfect time to take a break and refocus your thoughts. A strategy I used to divert my attention away from Esperanza was when I gave Esperanza to my first editor, I already had the questions, concerns and thoughts of where I wanted the story to go before my editor finished so that I can compare to his thoughts and what he did. So by doing this prior to having the editor edit Esperanza during the period of free time I had I was able to just focus on other writing projects.

Without naming the projects I now have on the shelf waiting to be developed into a final draft worth publishing are manuscripts for five books. These books are in their infancy, just raw blueprints I have for when I commit to them 100%. I also have outlines, and notes for multiple projects as well, and three screenplays. It sounds like a lot but these were all created and developed during the 10 years I spent writing Esperanza.

So don't fear going off the main path every now and then. Not only is it a way to take a break from your priority project but it is a productive way to take the ideas for other projects brewing in your mind and begin to mold it into something, create the foundation so that it is ready to be built on when the time comes.

Getting lost, looking within, spending more time alone

If you really want to get to know yourself better and more, spend more time alone. There is nothing wrong with being alone, in fact, I feel that not enough people do it, or spend enough time alone. We live in an extrovert's world, where we feel we have to constantly be with or around people, and be very loud and proud, even if you don't have a clue what you're talking about. That's the world we live in, a world where everyone is together and happy as can be, but are we really as human beings. We are programed to believe that we have to be with people all the time, and if you are quiet, shy, a loner, or someone who isolates themselves from the chaotic world these type of people are quickly judged as being strange, a weirdo, a recluse, someone who needs psychiatric help, someone plotting the next school shooting or public bombing, or a domestic terrorist or ISIS recruit.

I am an introvert, I am quiet, shy, and at times a loner, and every negative label that these people get, I had people say about me. So, yeah, being quiet, shy, a loner, a Pisces, and being into alternative media/investigative journalists/conspiracy theories, really gets people looking at you in a negative manner.

Here I am though. Somehow I was good enough to play on a national championship college soccer team, graduate from college, and write and publish Esperanza. So, how can that be? Even after graduating from college, during the ten year period I spent writing Esperanza, and early drafts of my published books and future projects, as an employee I was also looked down upon as the strange one, who kept to himself, who would be laughed at for the way I look, dress, and for being me, walked by without even a hello or a look in the eyes. Questioned for being the first person at work every day, because I chose to in order to get some writing done.

It's sad but the world we live in is a processed, programed hive. The mass of people considered to be the norm of society, the 9-5 hardworking Joes and Janes, who act like the adult children portrayed on T.V. shows or reality T.V., who do live way beyond their means, and complain about everything and everyone in the world, who indulge in negativity. Oh yeah, they also expect everyone to bow down to them, and live in a bubble of a world where everything is about them. So, yeah, I can see why in the world we live in today someone like me is considered to be strange.

As David Icke said, we are born in a mad house, and when you wake up and realize this and try telling people we live in a mad house, you as the awaken soul are told that you're crazy. That's how I've always seen the world, and that's how I see it to this day. I'm not a trendy progressive or someone who has to constantly check their social media. In fact I didn't have a Facebook account until I published Esperanza in 2017. Even now as a published author even though there are some social media sites I've created accounts on in order to get exposure and reach out to fans of my work, still it's a bit uncomfortable for me at times even though I have broken out of my introvert shell at this point.

So, getting away from the insane world we live in, to spend time alone is healthy. The mind, body and soul needs it, and when you do break away from the insane asylum, you can begin to see it for what it is, and start to see who you really are, and not the "Phantom Self," this caricature, programed persona a majority of people become.

Sitting in a café for hours, going for long walks with no direction, running, exercising, yoga, driving around for an hour or so, or simply being in the comforts of your own home without using any electronics or doing anything at all. Just sitting or pacing around in a meditative state, reflecting or going over the many thoughts that pass through the mind is a healthy way of spending some alone time. It can be refreshing and also inspiring. Some of my best ideas come from just being alone.

Adapting to a new way of living

"Love and marriage, love and marriage, they go together like a horse and carriage . . . " Yeah that sounds right. There is nothing wrong with marriage, it's an awarding journey to take in life, but like any journey there are mountains to climb, tides to sail, and wounds to heal. It's a battlefield with the threat of war out breaking at any moment. As a struggling independent writer, who had a set schedule and routine before engaging in marriage, it at first was suffocating. I went from having all the time in the world to write, to having that time cut into half. I had to balance my time between being with my wife and writing.

Not only did I have to find time to write, but I was now working on building a life with my wife. My focus was being diverted towards other things such as setting up a proper wedding in a church, helping her with lawyers, getting her residence documents, finding a job, building her Solanoexp business, being supportive when she gets home sick, and finding peace and love on the uncommon ground an Aries and Pisces walk on.

In the beginning it was tough, but no matter how frustrating it got at times, I was able to make time to write, and get myself into the right state of mind. And no matter how many confrontations we've had, Gabriela always believed in me, and I needed that since no one in my life seemed to or seemed to care at all that I was writing a book and pursuing the life of an independent writer. She had the same entrepreneurial work ethic and vision as I.

"Life is stranger than fiction." I met my wife in the café I wrote Esperanza in. After spending 4 years developing and writing about my protagonist Gabriela from Mexico, the real life Gabriela from Mexico came walking into my life. Thoughts manifest reality and Gabriela, my wife is the manifestation of my imagination. The law of attraction is magical and I have proven it to be true.

She is the strongest woman I know, with the heart of a lion and the soul of an angel; she pushes me to be a better human being. Without her I wouldn't be where I am now. Her entrepreneurial spirit blankets me with the positive mentality and will power to succeed and strive beyond imagination with my writing and life. She's the jack boot that kicks me in the ass when needed and the loving support to get me there.

So the forbidden path of marriage I used to never imagine nor want to walk down has been rewarding. This sacred bond makes me a better man and fuels my writing. Beside every successful man there is a great woman and Gabriela is not only the kryptonite to my heart but my cosmic angel bride; my guide and light.

And then there was life . . . my new inspiration

February 20, 2015 my greatest gift was born, Sofia. The birth of my daughter was not only a wonderful moment in my life, but also the beginning of a transitional phase as well. I was now a father. The first year of being a father would not only be rewarding, but a challenge as well. I had to find a way to be a husband, a father, and continue to write and pursue the life of an independent writer.

I didn't sulk or give up; once again, I had to find time to write, and I did. I wasn't going to give up on Esperanza, especially at this point in my life since I was near the end. I was now working with an editor, and focused on finalizing a final draft. The story was now set in stone, along with the characters, and I needed to mold it into a final product.

Every time I looked into Sofia's eyes she made me feel alive. I wanted to live for her and she gave me the drive to finish Esperanza. Everything I did was for her and the pursuit of living life as a full-time independent writer was now pursued with different priorities. It was no longer about me making it to live this free spirited traveling life as an indie writer, but to be successful enough so that I can provide for her, give her a better life and inspire her to chase dreams as she grows older.

Almost done

"The book is almost done," is what I seemed to constantly tell myself and others. It became a catch phrase to laugh about, and others would time and time again ask me when is the book going to be done. I knew when it was going to be done, but I felt like Michelangelo, when Pope Sixtus IV would constantly nag him, and ask him when he was going to finish painting the Sistine Chapel, and Michelangelo would reply, "When I can." It will be finished, when it's finished, that's how I saw it. The book, Esperanza, would be done when it's done. When it would be done, I didn't have an exact date, but I did have an exact time frame. I knew that as I got near the end I was pushing to have it done by the summer of 2017, which would be the 10 year anniversary since the time I started writing Esperanza, (June 2007), until the time I finished writing the first draft (August 2007).

The writing process is long and grueling, but one thing I always did was set little goals to achieve along the way. Every year from 2007-2017 I would create a list of tasks I would need to complete by the end of the year. Some would be weeklong goals to reach, others would be a month long goals, or a seasonal goals (2-4 months). Whatever the goal was I was focused on I stuck with it. It was either editing and rewriting certain chapters, or parts of the story, adding in new chapters or characters, rearranging chapters, taking chapters out and writing new ones, or just simply reading the story, over and over again, and taking out unnecessary content, or narrative.

No matter what it was I was focused on I had a game plan, made a very strict schedule and end goal for myself, and I stuck with it. This work ethic, as mentioned before I developed from the years I played soccer. All this came natural to me, and I sometimes felt real bad for people I've spoken to about this, who just didn't understand or couldn't do what I did, especially people who were also trying to write, or people who said they were going to begin some sort of business venture. It's funny I look back now, at how I was with writing Esperanza, being very grounded, focus, and strong willed, determined to finish and succeed, and a majority of people I would see often or speak to about writing my book, either looked or spoke to me as if I was crazy or something was wrong with me, or they would speak to me in a mocking manner as if I was someone who couldn't do what I was attempting to do or it was just some short term wishful thinking hobby. I still to this day find it funny how the ambitious ones, who go beyond the limits an ordinary, average person would never attempt to partake, are the subject of ridicule by the people who have no desire, or will to achieve greatness. Throughout history this has been going on, and still to this day the dreamers, the innovators, the ones who create something from nothing, get mocked, laughed at, or told their crazy, yet, the persecutors seem to have no ambition or desire to chase dreams or they are fearful of pursuing what is burning in their heart. These same people are also the ones who end up buying products of the dreamers they mock or do not understand, and/or try to emulate them.

So as far as being almost done, I think that is a term I will continue to use until the day I die. Esperanza is done, but there are many, many more books, and stories to be told, and other ventures and projects I have planned for the future. My life and all I want to, and will create is in constant motion, and will always be a work in progress that is almost done.

Trust in your editor

Your editor will be like your sparring partner. He or she will attempt to beat the shit out you and your dreams. This is necessary in order to grow as a writer, and help your book be molded and transformed into a polished up, final product. The truth hurts, but it is needed, and will make your book better than what it was, or at least what you thought it was.

I had two editors help me with Esperanza. The first editor I met in the café I would use as my office to write Esperanza. It was a fateful encounter, and we hit it off right from the very beginning. CVT was a dean of professors at a College, who had a PHD and had written and published books, and had edited books of numerous authors, one of them was Toni Morrison. So, I was fortunate to have met CVT who showed interest in my book and in me. From the very beginning he knew he was dealing with an amateur writer, and boy did he let it be known. He criticized me on everything, from the way it was written, the structure, the language, and even the fact that I don't read enough novels. The good thing was that he had the same interest in films as I, and enjoyed the same films I did, and understood how my story was being written in this Robert Rodriguez, Quentin Tarantino manner. He loved the plot, especially my dialogue, and said that my dialogue was the strongest part of my book, and that I had compelling narrative, that needed to be cut down, tightened and written with less stage direction and repetitiveness.

I worked with CVT for two years, and he had helped me grow as a writer, and Esperanza grow and evolve as well. He pushed me, pushed me every time to write better, and he was the bad medicine that I needed. After CVT and I parted ways, I now had an updated draft that was ready to be read and critiqued, but by who. I knew I wanted to give it to someone who didn't know me personally, but also someone I could trust. The first person I gave my manuscript to, to read was a woman from my apartment building, who worked in production in Hollywood, who I have met and spoken to a handful of times. She seemed nice, and understood stories. So I gave her my manuscript. The next three months would be stressful. She was not as reliable as I thought. She never answered her phone, never responded to text messages, and dodged me every time I got ahold of her. I wasn't sure if this lady was taking my manuscript and going about trying to publish it on her own, working with her Hollywood production buddies behind my back and without my consent, or who knows what, hopefully not losing it and having it fall into the wrong hands. The worse scenarios played out in my mind, until finally she told me, in an angry manner, that she's been sick, can't walk, and couldn't read the manuscript in the duration of time I wanted it. I remember meeting her to get my manuscript back. She had nothing but harsh words for me, "Good luck trying to get that published, it's too big." And that was it, I moved on.

I sat on this updated final draft for one year. From summer of 2015 to the summer of 2016 I didn't look at Esperanza at all. I worked on other writing projects, with hopes of finding someone reliable and trustworthy to read and critique Esperanza. Once again fate would bring someone into my life. At another café I write at, a gentleman I frequently see, struck up a conversation with me. When I revealed I was an aspiring writer, he told me about a friend of his, who was in business and just finished writing a book. He hooked me up with her.

The cosmic order and fate were on my side. CC was just the right person. She had a lovely personality, had a business mind set, enjoyed reading, and was willing and determined to help me out. We set up a time frame and after four months she was able to read my entire manuscript and give a very honest, and thorough critique. It was all I was looking for and needed. Her feedback confirmed flaws I already noticed, or didn't which needed to be fixed, and her praise gave me the confidence to carry on to the publishing process. I would take the critique draft of Esperanza, do all the necessary rewrites and edits, and begin to seek one final professional editor to polish it up into a final draft ready to be published.

ED would be the professional editor who would polish Esperanza up into a publish ready final draft. I discovered her via an indie writer association website, which had a watchdog list of editors and publishers. Based on her profile and her pricing she was the perfect person. At first, I admit it, I felt as if I was being scammed, that I just wired all this money to this editor who I didn't know at all, didn't know what she looked like either, only that she got a great rating on the watchdog list, but in the end she was the best thing for me. She took the edited draft that I had from CVT, and helped to trim it down more to a readable size. She also gave some great advice, which helped me mold Esperanza into a final draft to be published, and helped me become a better writer.

Final draft

I now had a final draft that was ready to be published. Since I started writing Esperanza I always knew that I was going to publish it independently. At the time I didn't know how I was going to do it, but then I heard about a publishing service, Authorhouse. So, as I spent the many years writing Esperanza, Authorhouse was going to be the service platform I was going to use. I reviewed and looked over the process on their website numerous times, spoke to consultants from the business, and even mapped everything out financially, which was going to cost a lot, more than what I spent on my editors. Fortunately for me, the independent writer I met, when I began writing Esperanza, who told me it took her 13 years to write and publish her book, I just happened to run into as I was looking for a final editor. She was excited that I finally finished my book, and was getting ready to publish, and when I told her I was going to use Authorhuse as she did, she became bitter and warned me not to. Well, Authorhouse who she published with turned out to be a money making business that cares less about its writers. They not only over charged people to publish their book, but based on her experience; they don't pay writers the royalties they earn. Also, after I spoke to her, I did some deeper investigating and found nothing but bad reviews about the Authorhouse business, saw that they were red flagged on the indie writer association watchdog website I discovered. This was great news, knowing this before I would go ahead and publish with them, but now what. I spent 10 years writing, anticipating using the Authorhouse services to publish, and now I had no independent platform to publish with. Fortunately after the independent writer forewarned me about Authorhouse she recommended I use Createspace.

So, I investigated Createspace and other independent publishing services. I narrowed it down to three, and I ended up using Createspace. To me based on the services they provided, royalties percentage, and the layout of the site, it suited me. As I was prepping to do modifications to my manuscript, I spent a lot of time learning about Createspace, how it works, how to use it, reading about and watching and listening to other writers on YouTube who used Createspace and educating myself about how to utilize Createspace as a published author.

The end . . .well, not yet, time to modify

The modifications of a novel and a manuscript should be the last thing that you think about, well, that's at least what I thought. If I could do it all over again, I would have spent more time on writing my manuscript on a modified file that was ready to be put into a Createspace template, or sent off to a publisher based on their modification standards. Even though in total I spent about two months modifying, and molding my final edited manuscript into the final document file needed to be sent off for publishing, it was a FUCKING PAIN IN THE ASS! IT FUCKING SUCKED!

So with that said, make sure to at least look into how you want your book to be published regarding, what size. Out of all the different sizes a published book could be, it's best to know which one you want to publish your book as ahead of time, so you could set up all the margins, word and line spacing, paragraph alignments etc.

The beauty about using Createspace is that they provide a modified Word template based on a variety of book sizes. The problem that I had was that when I pasted my unmodified file onto the template I had to manually modify everything, from the font size, to the paragraph alignments and spacing. What really sucked was having my final draft, Word file manuscript, more than double in size when I pasted it onto a book size Word doc. My final draft went from 445 pages to about 650 pages. I ended up with a fucking BEHEMITH. All my chapter beginnings, and paragraphs were all over the place, and nothing was spaced out properly. So I had to find a clever way to get my monster to at least fit into a 6x9 book template, without stepping outside the standard book modifications guidelines.

So, I played around with different font sizes, and ended up going under the recommended minimum, which is 11pt font. I took a bold risk and went with a 10pt font in order to get my book to be a somewhat reasonable size, which ended up being a 6x9 568pg book, which is about the size of a good hardcover book. This was my first published book, and I'm an easy go with the flow of things kind of person, who was just happy to get my book published. And to my surprise, the 10pt font wasn't that bad on printed paper. And when I received my proof, it was just PERFECT. IT LOOKED GREAT. A hell of a lot better than what I thought it would look like on the printed book. So based on this experience never feel held back due to all the standards of the literary world. Like I said from the very beginning, there is no right or wrong way to write a story and publish a book. Just do what you feel is right, and looks good to you. That was my philosophy from the very beginning all the way up to the very end when I was finally published.

And to be honest at first one of the things that scared me after my book was published was that no one was going to buy it because of the price, which was $19.45 due to the size of the book. On Createspace you can price your book, but they give you a price range based on the size of your book. My book was on the high end. It was for a high price, something I felt would scare buyers away for not being a hardcover book, but a paperback book from an unknown author. But then again, I didn't care, I was published, and being published is worth more than any price tag. And so as I have always planned from the very beginning, since I am an unknown author, my marketing had to be different and clever, without selling out. And with the big price tag I had, I had to focus on my original intent which was to create buzz about my book, and myself.

10 years . . . published, marketing, shameless self-promotion

Now that 10 years have come and gone, and I am now published there is this sense of relief, but also a sense of knowing that I'm not finished yet. The physical phase of Esperanza is complete, and now I must begin the social media, marketing phase.

Being social has been my weakness, and anxiety. It has haunted me for most of my life, and now having to go from this quiet, shy, anti-social, awkward person, and attempt to become this "Hey, look at me," social media personality, was in the beginning a strange transformation. So, instead of diving into the social media world, I went back to one of those people who have inspired me as an artist, Trent Reznor.

Not only have I been a fan of Trent Reznor, and Nine Inch Nails, but he has been the artist I could relate to and admire. Throughout the early years of his career he was dealing with social anxiety. He kept out of the limelight as much as he could, and rarely did any interviews or appearances on talk shows, or some red carpet event. That was the old Trent Reznor, who I related to, and then as the world seemed to be burning and falling apart, Trent Reznor, as I, began to come out of his eggshell. His lyrics were becoming more political, and he was now involved with the film making process, scoring movies, winning an Oscar, and all over social media. He had his way of doing it, and what I admire most about him, especially as a musician, he was one of the big names in the music industry, who during the millennium, and whole Napster, music stealing/streaming era, kept quiet, sat back and waited to see what happened with this new phase in music. He embraced it and developed new innovative ways to connect with fans and distribute his music.

I learned many things from Trent Reznor during this time, way before I even thought of writing Esperanza. Instead of getting furious, and complaining that people are stealing his music, and he's not making any money, Trent eventually came out and said that releasing free music is a good thing, it's inevitable. In this new technological era, people are more connected than ever before, and if you connect with fans on a personal level, they will always support you, even if they can get your music for free. People still want to have that physical product, it's just now about how you connect with them, and the approach to how fans can get the physical product, and what makes them want to have it; Limited Edition.

Trent Reznor perfected this marketing plan. People are now listening to digital, so they need reason to buy something physical. So Trent Reznor would put out new limited edition CDs. This created a want mentality, especially amongst true fans. There would be an x amount of CDs and each one would be individually numbered. He would also, every now and then sell signed personal items. And now what has been playing and working out in Trent Reznor's favor is the return of Vinyl. His generation used Vinyl. It is a part of his music, and now its back.

I'm not a musician, and I don't have a solid fan base, with many books, (not yet), but what I do know, and what has worked for me is attempting to connect with followers the best I can, without selling out, or trying too hard. Although I am now out on social media I still try to keep this mystique, as did Trent Reznor in the early years, and post every so often, making sure each post has meaning.

Along with the book, I have created some promotional prints and look forward to creating t-shirts, and other merchandise that connects with the book, and see what happens. There are no limits.

From the very beginning when Myspace, Facebook, and all the other social media sites began popping up I had no interest in creating a profile and becoming a part of the trendy social media craze. When I finally became published I knew that I needed to become a part of those worlds in order to get my book out there, and connect with a mass of people. After signing up with Facebook and creating an account, I felt sick by the end of the day. I wasn't use to the constant updates popping up on my cellphone and laptop Facebook page I had opened. It was exhausting to see all of these people reaching out to me, leaving comments, and then me having to respond, even when I had nothing to say.

It's strange to me sitting before my laptop, and watching every 10-30 seconds a red number flashing at the top of my screen indicating that someone liked something I posted, wrote a comment, or someone friended me. I guess I'm supposed to feel all good and gooey inside, but, nah, I feel sick in the head. My head still hurts. I think that all this exposure is shutting down my sense of consciousness, and free flowing thoughts I use to have in my head. Now I understand what a mind trap/prison feels like.

One marketing technique which I thought about doing many years before I would finish and publish Esperanza was to leave dummy books in bookstores, cafes, or in a busy park. The first time I did this was October 1, 2017 in New York City. I went into the city on a beautiful, clear brisk autumn day with my wife and my daughter to see The Very hungry Caterpillar theater show in a small theatre next to Union Square Park. Ironically, the famous Barnes and Noble on the north side of the park, was one of the many book stores I would go to, and dream of having my book in someday. It was also a strategically mapped out location I would use to leave dummy books.

So I brought a bunch of my books with me on that day, and went into the Barnes and Noble. I placed a bunch real neat on the Must Read Fiction shelf, with all the must read books, and then I put some on the New Paper Back fiction shelf next to some popular books at the time. My goal was just to have the books be seen, read, and thought about by the many random people who would go into the book store that day. Whatever happened to those books, or who read them I don't know, but imagine that at least one person was curious enough to read through it, talk about it, and maybe even attempt to buy it. And if they weren't able to buy it, then it will probably just be placed on a book shelf for all eternity, for others to find and read, which is ok with me, because in time, my goal was to have many people see it, read it and talk about it. This was my way of creating some buzz.

I also left a book on a bench in Washington Square Park. I tried to do it stealthily so that no one would see me, and then try to warn me that I left my book. I didn't have to worry, because no one paid any attention to me, or the book I left. I went back to the same spot hours later and saw that my book was still there. I guess people were scared to take it, because they weren't sure whose book it was, but I'm sure during the whole day, at least one person had the audacity to pick it up and read, or pass it on to someone else.

What has actually benefitted me was just talking to people about my book and being an indie author, it worked and those people ended up buying my book. I would be at a café, or at a party and having a conversation with someone I don't even know about who I am, and what I do, and the moment I mention I am an indie author and I'm published they become fascinated. I then engage in talking about my book and the writing process and this creates this truth that people connect with and are willing to support.

So for me to engage with people and speak with them on a human level works. As of now I have some internet radio show interviews set up and plan on doing some speaking events about my book, the writing process and life as an indie author in the near future. I plan on building off of this and create a modest fan base that will support me and become devoted followers of my work and as an indie author. I hope to entertain, educate and inspire.

The reality of writing a book

The idea of writing a book is one of those thoughts that cross many people's mind. Some people are willing to take the challenge of acting on those thoughts, while others play around with the idea and fantasize about how "I could write a book about this." For those who enjoy reading books all they see is the book and not what it took to create it. This is the reality of writing a book.

Therefore, this is for the bold ones who choose to take that journey of writing a book and for those who are thinking about it at the moment. At first the idea of writing a book may sound "COOL" and the idea of being a published author may seem "SEXY." The reality is that writing a book isn't "cool" and being a published author isn't "sexy". Writing a book could feel like driving without your hands on the wheel on a suicide mission through hell and becoming a published author can be lonely at times, but it is also basically becoming an established writer, and better person than before; mainly due to the process and accomplishing such a feat.

If you are considering writing a book this is for you. The percentage of people who actually write a book is small. A reason for this is once the reality of what is necessary to write a book sets in, the burden, the time it will take, and/or the commitment isn't there, many people give up and quit, or they race through a book and pump out something that isn't any good or not what it could have been. Patience is one of many vital virtues to have if you consider writing a book.

For those who are aspiring to write a book or have already begun to, here is a little bit of advice based off of my own experience of writing a book. It took me 10 years to write my first novel, Esperanza and no matter how difficult it got, burdensome it became, and how much I wanted to quit, I never caved in and gave up. I carried on no matter how treacherous the road became.

Along the way not only have I become a better writer but I have grown as a human being. The writing process changes you like never before. There is something magical about writing and that conscious and unconscious connection made with creating something from nothing, building a story, or any kind of book with words, and making that channeling connection with your higher self and sometimes downloading information from the unseen, the universal consciousness we can sometimes all tap into.

With that said if you are to dive in and make the attempt, make sure that you're willing to make a 100% commitment, anything less will make the journey difficult, not of the worth it could be, and you'll just be wasting your time. You will need to be discipline with the balance of your life, writing process and daily writing routine. Being adaptable to sudden changes with life, the process and with the writing will be essential. Also without having a strong work ethic and being able to maintain time management with your life, work, and writing you'll end up creating minimal work and begin to get lost in life and with your writing.

It's a lonely road, not many people are willing to take and if you dare to, be sure to find yourself on a path no one will understand but you. Yes, others will be needed to help along the way such as editors, beta readers, formatters, other authors and their advice, for some mentors, writer's groups, friends and family, informative books, podcasts, and Youtube videos of people talking about the writing process, writing a book, and everything in between. In the end though it is just you and the idea you have brewing in your mind which you attempt to write and turn into a book. Protect and nourish your ideas like your children, because when your book is published, it will feel like having your child. Last when writing it is just you, your ideas, and a blank sheet of paper.

Getting Started: The Writing Roadmap

So you want to write a book? Well, as with most things in life the hardest part is to start, and the question is; where to begin?

1. Visualize.

Before even writing you need to think about a story you want to tell or a character you want to bring to life. You need to visualize both and manifest it in your mind. Spend a good amount of time doing this. This is the fun part where there are no rules, boundaries or regulations. Anything is possible and anything you imagine has the potential to grow and evolve into something great. This is where the seed is planted. This is where the dreams begin to manifest.

2. Manifest your thoughts.

After thinking about your story and character the next step to do is to now get all those thoughts down on paper. Write it all down. There is really no right or wrong way of doing this but what worked for me was first write out what the plot is in 1 paragraph, next divide the story up into three parts, beginning, middle and end and write a paragraph about each part. From there you can now begin to break the story down into chapters and start outlining the entire book, chapter by chapter. These could be 1-3 sentences, brief descriptions. As for the character/characters don't put too much thought into who they are at this stage, because they will evolve and change during the writing of the story. The idea at this stage is to just empty your thoughts out, like a child dumping a box of Legos onto the floor, organizing them and beginning to build.

3. Building a frame.

The first two stages will act more like blueprints at this point. They will be your guide as you dive into actually writing the story. What worked for me and what I recommend is to just dive into the story, just start writing without worrying about structure, fancy words, spelling, grammatical errors, or how good or bad it is. Just write because when you finish your first draft by the time you get it published the story will have changed completely. Your job at this stage is to just beat out the entire manuscript. How long this takes is up to you and your life, work, writing balance. Usually a 300 page book could be written in what is the equivalent of a season, 3-4 months.

4. Balance.

The key to successfully writing a book is all about balance, how do you balance your life, work, and writing. If you are serious about writing a book you will have to find and make time to write each day. There are 24 hours in a day so there should be no excuses why you can't devote at least 1 hour a day writing. Even if you are only able to write one paragraph or one sentence, it is progress and each day it will grow. Set a writing schedule and stick with it.

5. Reflect.

Congratulations, at this point you should have completed your first draft. The next thing to do, is to let your manuscript sit untouched for some time. This could be for 1-2 weeks, a month, or even what I have done before 1 year. Why? It's a healthy habit to master because as it sits, you can relive the story, think about it, the changes you want to make and it helps clear your mind of all the clutter, so that when you revisit it you'll see it from a different perspective. How long you sit on it is up to you, but as you leave it alone, you should have someone read it to give you feedback, take notes on things you like, don't like, want to change, take out, add in, and last what I do is take this time to start thinking about and outlining another story I would like to write.

6. Repeat.

After letting it sit, having someone read it and critique it, and taking notes on all you would like to change, you can now go back, revisit the story and begin doing edits, rewrites and molding the story into something better. I recommend doing this 3 times before sending it off to a professional editor. You want the story to be solidified and most of the grammar to be on par with a final draft.

The final published book being held in your hands should be the big picture you see at the very beginning, this should be your motivation to just start writing. It's that simple. So don't be afraid to, you never know what it is you may end up creating and how many lives you could change, entertain and inspire with your words. It all starts with one word so start with just one word, start writing.

<u>10 Years</u>

It took me 10 years to complete my first novel Esperanza. Many notebooks were filled, many napkins and scraps of paper were written on, and many drafts were written, rewritten, and changed. During this ten year journey I was also dealing with and battling with the confines of life, internal and external obstacles, juggling multiple jobs, and dealing with and facing positive and negative people. And no matter how many times I wanted to quit because it got harder each day, I was faced with road blocks and failure, it seemed like a waste of time or wouldn't amount to anything or it seemed to never end, I never stopped. I kept writing even when there seemed to be nothing to write, I worked on other writing projects. Even when people with big egos, those who are quick to judge without knowing me personally or what I'm doing, the wicked ones who looked down upon me with pity, doubt, and disbelief still I carried on. Evil looks, hurtful words, or being laughed at used to bother me and affect my emotions and decisions, not anymore. The 10 years I spent writing Esperanza not only made me a stronger person mentally and in the heart but also taught me many things about being human, chasing and achieving dreams/goals, and becoming successful and evolving as a spiritual being. Here are some of the basics I've learned, which have worked for me in life and as a writer.

Patience
Without it you'll break emotionally and give up too soon. You won't be able to see your true potential or that in others. You'll miss out on seeing the beautiful rose that grows from shit.

Discipline
Without structure, balance, and self-control you'll break during stressful situations. Discipline is what I learned from soccer, keeping fit physically and mentally, having a strict work schedule to develop my skills and character, and being prepared and able to overcome any

barriers and/or changes.

Vision

Being able to foresee your final destination; dreaming big yet focusing on the little paths and goals needed to overcome before reaching the big goal. You have to visualize each realistic and optimistic path and outcome. Like a chess player and a soccer player you have to see 4-6 moves/plays ahead from the present moment. This makes you prepared, one step ahead of an opponent/obstacle and better prepared to face failure, transition, and make the necessary moves to surpass your original intent.

Work ethic/time management

These two work together. Work ethic is what I learned from soccer. Training/writing everyday harder and knowing there is someone out there doing what I'm doing, has the same dreams and is pushing just as hard or harder to succeed. You have to push harder, to perfect your craft. You have to be better than not only those seeking the same dreams/goals but better than yourself each day. In order to work hard you need to manage your time. Create and follow a strict time schedule that fits in with your job, family time, free time, obligations, and any sudden event that occurs. Find and make time to write. When I was single I had all the time in the world. When I had a girlfriend then got married that time was split in half. When I had a daughter it was gone. So instead of giving up or sulking I made an effort to make time. When my wife was at work and I wasn't I wrote. When my wife and daughter were asleep late at night or in the early hours I wrote. When I had a 1-2 hour window of free time during the day instead of watching Netflix or surfing the internet I wrote. There are 24hrs in a day there are no excuses for not finding 1-2 hours a day to write or work on your dreams/goals.

Love

Love yourself, not in an egotistic manner but in being proud of who you are. Love what you are doing with your life or the dream you're chasing. Love those who are important to you whether it's family, friends, or people from all walks of life who somehow connect with you, respects you, and/or challenges and helps you grow as a human being. Love is the force which binds us, fuels us, and guides us, and will help you achieve your dreams and bring you happiness.

Believe

Believe in yourself. No matter how misguided the path you are on may seem, no matter how much advice or opinions you get from others, or from the so called experts, the only voice that will guide you in the right direction towards your final destination that you see fit for you and the only road that will take you there is YOURS. All the answers you need are in your heart, so trust that feeling of knowing, and go with it. It may fail or get you into trouble, but ultimately it's not only being true to yourself, but in the end you could look back at the journey you took with no regrets. Help, guidance, and advice from others is great, we need that in life. Teams are what win, not the individual, but ultimately in the end, it's the individual actions that make the character you are. Believe in yourself, and then others will believe in you, and come to you for help, for guidance, and advice.

Adaptability

Being adaptable as a human being is a necessary survival trait. It's how we evolved, and it's how you will be able to face change, failure, roadblocks, and anything else that gets in the way of your dreams/goals, and growth process. Being adaptable will enable you to be able to face any challenges without fear or excuses, such as being unprepared and enable you to overcome any feat and achieve greatness.

Be Positive

There are a lot of negative people in the world. There will always be someone out there speaking negative about you, who won't like you for some reason, either because of the way you live your life, or the way you look. There will be negative people who won't agree with you or believe in you. Sometimes they will be direct, use social media, or other times they will gossip with the flock of negative hive mind people that reflect who they are, and try to rally up an uneducated, programed, blindly misguided zombie mass of people to go against you and all you believe in. That's the sick world we live in. We see this everyday on the News, on T.V shows, in the media, in magazines, on the internet, in the office, in the schools, in any sort of work place, in arenas and stadiums or gathering ground where there are people. DON"T GET SUCKED INTO THIS NEGATIVE WORLD OR WAY OF BEING. This negative mentality and negative people will bring you down, and divert you from your dreams/goals. Even when times are tough stay positive, and carry on, there will always be brighter days ahead. Leave behind negative people and influences; they are the cancer of the human race.

Part II

<u>On Writing</u>

101 Quotes/Tips/Thoughts

In this section is a collection of personal quotes, tips, and thoughts regarding the writing process which I've developed and utilized, during the 10 years I spent writing Esperanza. Everything you will find in this section I based off of my experiences and all I've learned. It was a growing period as a writer and I wish to share all of my knowledge with you.

For any aspiring writer, the unknown which awaits you after writing that first word can be scary, but having someone who has been there before to guide you can be inspiring. I wish to inspire you as you venture down the indie author's path. Here's a little bit of magic that worked for me, I hope it does magic for you, so, good luck as you begin your journey.

<u>1</u>

Write often, even if you have nothing to write.

Having nothing to write is so common with the average writer and for anyone who is trying to write something. Writer's block sucks. Having nothing to write when you need to write is one of the worse feelings a writer could have. We usually feel useless or become overwhelmed with anxiety. For those who are not trying to write a book it may be a paper, report, or e-mail that needs to be written ASAP and sometimes during those moments there is nothing on your mind to write.

Therefore being in the habit of writing often will condition you to write when you have nothing to write. Having something written down is better than having nothing. Even if it is just one word, that one word could be just as powerful as 500 words.

For all the writers out there and all who struggle with writing, get in the habit of writing often. You'll be amazed at the thoughts you can get down when you look back on all you've written when you had nothing to write.

2

Turn your writing into a habit. Make it a daily activity even if you write just one meaningful word a day.

Habits can be that which brings us down or builds us up. It is wise to break bad habits and invest in good habits. Therefore in order to become a successful writer or become better with your writing it needs to become part of your daily routine. You need to get into the habit of writing daily and often.

By conditioning yourself to write each day, even if just for a few minutes this habit will turn into a routine which will eventually grow into a conditioned habit that will grow.

It's the process which needs to be developed and the commitment. Just the way an athlete trains to be fit and better with their sport so is a writer each day by having the habit of writing daily and often.

Yes there will be days of not being in the mood or being in the right mind set. Even life and the world around can draw us away and break a good habit. That's ok, flow with it and try to get at least one word a day. Words are like magic so get in the habit of developing your craft and create some magic daily. You never know who you may touch or inspire.

<u>3</u>

Write for what you love and not for an audience. Your writing will become more authentic, and an audience will discover and connect more with you.

Writing should always come from the heart and nowhere else. The love that comes from within is more powerful than any external influences. This is why it is so important to write what you love and not for an audience.

Yes, there are writers and individuals who write for an audience. Some may become successful and make careers, but is it the right way for you? Is it authentic?

For me as a writer I feel the need to write what I love, be authentic and versatile; all with love from my heart. By being myself, being authentic and sharing what I love an audience has discovered and found me. Write what you love and you'll be surprised with how many people connect with.

<u>4</u>

Know that there will be days when you may end up staring at a blank page of paper for hours and not get one word written. As frustrating as those moments may be know that there will be days when words will flow out on to pages like brush strokes and hours will feel like minutes, and pages will be filled with words.

Every writer has experienced that moment of staring at a blank page for what seems like an eternity and write nothing. This moment sucks. It's depressing and can lead to negative thoughts.

As with all moments in life there are times of burden and times of joy, knowing this can help with getting past the blank page. And when those days of inspiration come words will magically flow out.

These are the moments when a writer's true integrity is tested. Be the writer that conquers the blank page, be the writer that strives.

<u>5</u>

Not everyone will like what you write. That is ok. Do not worry about the opinions of others only be concerned about that which is in your heart and continue to write no matter what the critics of your work say.

Worrying about the opinions of others will devalue your writing; it will hold you back on your true potential. There are billions of people in the world, its ok if some of those people dislike what you write, because out of the billions and the minority that dislike your work, the percentage of people out there who will like what you write is vast.

Negative words can be like cancer but to worry about the opinions of others is like being trapped in a prison. Instead of breaking free and writing what's in your heart, worrying about the opinions of others will keep you locked up in your cell of conformity thinking about writing what is politically correct, the norm, trendy, or the new fad instead of creating something new and original. All great pieces of work were at one time considered to be not good, or of any worth or crazy. Don't allow your crazy idea to not have the opportunity to blossom into something great.

<u>6</u>

Write with passion, not with obligations to serve others.

That which is created with passion will always have more value than content pumped out for someone else and not that which is in your heart.

Passion is the life force which drives us. Use that positive energy to create beautiful writing and pieces of art. Yes there are times when we are obligated to serve others but don't allow the conviction of this to bog down your process and suppress the passion you use when you are writing something that you love.

The process should always be fueled with passion no matter what the emotional state of being is either. Go with it and get it out, then will all of those obligations become something of worth and want. Always love what you are writing or doing, the actions reflect you and passion will always get your there.

<u>7</u>

Create a writing schedule that best suits your life.

Having balance with your life will enable you to conquer writing each day. There are 24 hours in a day so there is no excuse for finding time to write. Even if you write for just 20 minutes that will all add up if you write a little bit each day. It could be in the early hours of the day, in the afternoon, or late at night. That is up to you and what works with your life.

Therefore treat your writing like a job, a job you love so having a set schedule which suites your lifestyle is essential. Finding this time by balancing out your life, work, family time, and free time is necessary if you want to take writing seriously and do it full time.

Scheduling your writing sessions around your life will eventually turn into habit. After following this routine schedule you will find that when you do sit down to write it will all flow out.

<u>8</u>

Having a strong work ethic and time management are vital to becoming a successful writer.

As with anything in life if you don't put any effort into that which you are attempting it will not be of any worth. Having a strong work ethic with your writing is just as essential as the work an elite athlete puts into their training. You have to condition your writing, nurture it and put in the time. Even on the days when you may feel tired, or not in the mood, try to put in at least 20 minutes. Every minute adds up.

Use your time efficiently, manage your time. Time management is just as important as the effort you put into your writing. Managing the time you write with the time you spend each day with your job, family, life obligations, and down time is just as important. As much as writing should be a part of your life if writing is your passion and desire to do full time, don't allow it to interfere with your life, and vice versa. Make it work and put in the hard work needed to master the craft of writing. It can be done with discipline, time management and the will power to work on what you love, which is writing all you behold inside.

<u>9</u>

Have persistence. Everyone works at a different pace and nothing great was created in one week, or a month. Writing a novel takes a lot of effort and time.

Those who say they can write a book; great I wish you all the best. Those who think a quality book could be written in 1-3 months and have never written book before; let me know how that is going in 4 months.

Anyone can write a book but, not everyone has the persistence it takes to actually write one. Writing a book is a grueling process not many are willing to take or attempt especially after the truth of what it takes to write one is revealed. If you are bold enough to attempt to great but don't think that it has to be done in a few months or a year. Nothing great in life was created or made quickly. It takes time and patience.

The pace at which you work is up to you. Whether you are the tortoise or the hare, it really doesn't matter, unless you have deadlines. Work hard, with effort, at a steady pace best suited for you, persevere no matter what barriers you face and yes you could write a book. It's about the quality of the time you put into it not the speed at which you can pump out a book. Write, persevere, and stay on your own path.

10

Don't over think your first draft, just write and bang it out. The first draft is a blue print and it will not be the same story by the time you finish a final draft.

If you have an idea brewing in your mind, get it out before it dies. Yes writing a book takes time to do, but your first draft should be written at a steady pace with a goal of finishing it at most within a year. This will be your blue print. With this draft you will have your plot, main characters and conflict all set up to be analyzed when you revisit the story to do edits and rewrites. This will be needed to carry on with the story and turn it into a final draft.

The blue print is the guide you need to use to get to the end, a published book. Use it as your light and understand that what you have in the first draft will change or be omitted along the way. So don't spend too much time stressing over minor details. Have no attachments yet have love for it, the love you would have for a child. Remember letting go is true love so there should be no regrets in the end when letting characters go or pieces of written material you've spent hours writing, giving all your heart and soul to deleted and left behind. It is always for the better.

Just write and let the story flow out with the first draft. The blue print you create will shine in the end and the big picture will be seen on the open pages of your final draft and the published book will feel like a new born.

11

Sometimes ideas come from nowhere. If so, no matter how bad of an idea it may seem to be or strange, go with it and write it. You are one with the universe and the universe is always whispering to you.

Never silence the whispers of ideas that come from nowhere. Sometimes a story, a character, or a scene may manifest in our mind, and no matter how bad or crazy it may seem to be, don't let it fade away, water it and take a chance. Some of the strangest ideas can turn into some of the most brilliant pieces of work.

The universe within you is always connected with the unseen universe, the collective consciousness which is cluttered with ideas. When in tuned with this frequency some of the most magical ideas can manifest. Do not be afraid to recognize these ideas and flow with it. Write them down and watch them grow into something beautiful.

Sometimes writing can seem like channeling, like a clairvoyant connecting with unseen forces, so is a writer tapping into unseen ideas. This ocean of ideas is filled with dazzling and strange concepts waiting to be written. Catch these majestic tokens and be not afraid to create something amazing.

12

Once you start writing never stop, you'll live on forever with regret and will never know where the road may end.

It are the things in life we regret doing that we dwell on the most as we lay on our death bed. Don't let any idea or story die before you give it a chance to grow. No matter what it may blossom into, that road you take will always lead to something bright.

Every day we are going to be smothered with choices and chances to make. The same goes with the writing process. As a story is developing each word, sentence, character, scene, and the flow of the plot is faced with choices and decisions to be made. Some will be easier than others to execute. There will be times of doubt and the dreadful slump or writer's block phase may consume us.

Keep writing. Never stop. As treacherous as the road ahead may be, don't turn around and go down the avenue of regret. Regret of what could've been written will haunt you until the day you die, and the road ahead that may lead to something beautiful and fulfilling will never be seen

<u>13</u>

Once you finish writing your book and get it published it is not the end but only
the beginning to a new chapter filled with more commitment and obligations.
Just as you devoted yourself to writing it, you need to approach all aspects of
post publishing with the same passion.

This is usually the part of writing a book that most writers are delusional
about, fearful of, or have unrealistic expectations about. Marketing and self-
promotion is just as grueling as writing the book. It's a completely different
playing field, a field most writers are unfamiliar with.

As writers, especially writers writing their first book, a majority of our
focus is on the writing aspect. Yes we may think about a target audience, how
we will present ourselves and book on social media, but pitching your book and
yourself isn't something that comes natural to most writers nor is it something
most put a lot of thought into.

Marketing, pitching, and selling is an art form. It is a skill which is just as
important as writing. Most writers are introverts, shy, loners, who aren't usually
the life of a party or the "hey, look at me," kind of people. That's why we are
writers and that's why we should focus on the writing. The marketing process
can be taught, but the wise thing to do is to start marketing while writing your
book, learn the art and find professional marketers to help. In the end you need
to approach marketing with the same approach you do with writing, the process
never changes only the field.

<u>14</u>

Story Trumps compelling writing.

Yes, words can grab a reader and keep their attention, but when compared to the bigger picture is the story of any worth? Ultimately it is the story that the reader is interested in not the words, although the words play a crucial part. It is the story the reader becomes engaged with and is the reason a reader continues to read.

Words can be magical, words can be inspiring and motivating but it's the story (hopefully not the book cover) which gives a reader reason to lift up a book, open it up and desire to read it.

After reading a book or watching a movie it is the story that stands out the most to the audience, especially if it is a good one. Even if the two dance together on pages or the big screen the story will always take the lead.

There are many examples of books and movies where the writing aspect wasn't great but the overall story was extraordinary, and massively loved by audiences from around the world. The Da Vinci Code stands out to me, a book which won the hearts of a global audience with its story.

<u>15</u>

The process of writing is similar to the process of creating life.

At first an idea is conceived, then there is a long growing period within the womb manifesting on paper, and then in the end is the birth of a new book. Treat the writing process as you would during the 9 months of pregnancy and the finish book as you would care for a new born child. There is love and passion with each stage of the process.

All of life takes time to grow as does a book.

<u>16</u>

Always carry a notebook around, and never forget the pen.

For any serious writer a notebook is an essential tool which should always be handy. It is where all thoughts, ideas, memories, observations and notes are kept. It is a physical representation of our mind. Along with it should always be a pen. The pen is what brings all to life.

No matter where you go in life a notebook should always be with you or near. You never know when a brilliant idea or story may pop up into your mind. One of the worst feelings a writer can have is being in a situation where you have a great story idea and you're stuck somewhere without a notebook or a pen. Always have the two kept at your side; they will become your best friends.

Even better is after writing in a notebook, they are always great to go back to and revisit. You never know what treasures await you deep inside. Something you may have written which at the moment was of no worth, may, many months or years later be the gem you were looking for to complete a project or start something new.

<u>17</u>

Balance your time between writing, day job, life, family, and rest. There are 24 hours in a day; there is no excuse for not finding the time to commit to all even if just for an hour a day.

Time management is essential. It is a strong virtue all must possess if you are to commit full time to writing or any dream that you want to pursue. Never allow the confines of life to hold you back. The daily grind of life can be overwhelming; it can break people physically, emotionally and mentally. It can kill your dreams. Do not allow this.

With the understanding that there are 24 hours in a day, and taking the time to map out each day there should be no reason why you cannot find at least 1 hour a day to write. Even if you divide that time up it is ok. This then will help you develop a good habit which will eventually help you manage your life, job, family and rest time and create more writing time. It's up to you and the life you live. Do not try to emulate others' writing schedule but find what works best for you. Find the balance and you will discover success.

18

When editing and cutting down a book, at first it will feel wrong, like harming a loved one, but don't be afraid to rip it a part, it is for the better. Butcher the shit out of your own work for in the end it will be thinner and better than before.

This is the scary truth of the final phases of writing a book. The editing part can seem like a horror film; the suspense, the build up to something gruesome and scary and then that moment of truth, the bloody gore that becomes of slaying the beast, which in the end is for the better.

There are going to be characters, dialogue, scenes, phrases, sentences and pages of material that you might have spent hours, days and/or even months on developing, and then after all that, after having an editor look at all you have created you must now kill your baby. Breathe, let it settle, and then let it go, "LET IT GO," like the song goes. That is true love, letting go for the love of another; letting the bogged down material go. Once you break all emotional attachments, the hatchet in your sweaty palms won't feel as heavy; it will feel like fanning yourself with a hand fan on a beach on a hot summer day. This is paradise, this is what you want your final book to feel like and look like. LET IT GO.

<u>19</u>

Story ideas will come and go; always stick with the ones that never fade away.

Like dreams that fill your mind in the night so do story ideas; do not try to forget the ones that never fade away. No matter how bizarre or strange they may seem to be stick with them, they may have potential and develop into something magical.

There are reasons for such ideas to constantly reoccur. Even if it's your subconscious trying to tell you something, or if it's something psychological, never let it pass. Spend time with it and help it grow, you never know, it may be the seed you need to help you grow. It may be the story you've been looking for the one that will open up doors and bring you success.

<u>20</u>

Turn your writing into a habit, once it becomes engrained within you the writing process will become natural and you won't feel as if you have to force yourself to write. The process will just flow naturally as a river.

This is where you want to get as a writer. You want to be conditioned to just sit down and write naturally. All good writing comes from writing with ease. As with all fields in life, like a master pianist plays a solo concert, or a medical surgeon performs an 18 hour heart transplant, this is the type of ease and flow you want to develop as a writer.

It takes time and a lot of work. There will be many days of frustration and anger. This is natural and it will all come to pass. When the storm clouds do clear away and the waters become calm then will the river flow within you, and words will spill out onto the pages.

21

Never stress over what you can't control. There are millions and millions of books out there and other authors doing what you are doing. This should be the last thing you think about. Focus on you and what it is you are writing and then the universe will bring to you all that you need to strive along the way.

This is a fact; there are billions of published books out there in the world and millions of authors and other aspiring writers doing what you are doing. Understanding this fact and accepting it is crucial, but most importantly is having your own vision, and dream, your own path you want to take. Do not allow this fact to hold you back or discourage you, if anything it should fuel your fire and show you that if all those people can write a book so can you. Especially with knowing that there are some hack jobs out there, and terrible books that have been published; use this to get you moving even more.

Try to be yourself, be unique, be you. Fuck em', the last thing you want to do is to worry about what others have done and what others think. Yes, advice and opinions are needed along the way and will help you but don't get caught up with it and let it hold you back. Write for you and dream of being bigger than all those out there that have been published. Dream big, yet take realistic steps, and strive for greatness. There is plenty of space on the bookshelves for your books.

<u>22</u>

Outline. Do it during the beginning, do it during the editing and rewriting phase and do it again even after you finish your manuscript. Outlines are the blueprints you need to see the big picture of your story.

This is a process that should never fade away. From beginning to end this process is an essential way to organize your thoughts, and map out what ever section of your book you are writing. These will always be pieces to the puzzle that you can lay out before you and piece together however you want before executing it into a word file or document.

Visually it is always easier to see everything in pieces and will make the editing process go much smoother. Too many notes cramped together on a page, or pages of notes can bog you down or be overwhelming. Yes for some this may work and others may have their own way of outlining. For me though I outline with bullet points and short notes. This has worked for me and I hope that it shines some light on others who are not sure what approach to take when it comes to outlining.

23

Write from the heart and you'll succeed every time.

As with all matters in life love is the most powerful force. It drives us, it binds us and it fuels the heart. If there is any doubt in yourself or the work you produce, the heart will always bring you truth and that truth can never be smothered.

No matter what the outcome of a story is or what the critics think, the love written down from the heart will always find a way to connect with others, inspire, and uplift people with a beacon of hope. Even if your heart seems broken it can be mended together with the love from within, so write with love, the love of writing and the love you have for your characters and story, and love the process. Love from the heart is the only truth.

In the end, wherever the road takes you if it was written with the love from the heart there will be no regrets. Live life and love to write.

<u>24</u>

Anyone can write a book but not everyone can tell a compelling story.

The possibility for someone to write a book is there. However in order to write a compelling story that is up to the individual. It isn't something everyone can do. It takes a lot of time and effort. Even if it is a simple story, the amount of thought and detail put into a story is ultimately what will make it compelling.

Therefore it doesn't matter how many books a person can hack out, what it comes down to is how well written the story is. Writing a compelling story is an art not many people are willing to pursue. Nothing great in life happens without putting in the work. As with writing a compelling story, if that is the goal you set for yourself never settle for anything less, no matter how long it may take. Be the writer that stands above the rest, don't be the writer that is known for writing 100 books rather strive to be the writer known for writing a handful of compelling stories.

<u>25</u>

The internet is the greatest invention and asset to an independent author.

Use it to learn about the writing process, use it to research a book project, use it to learn about the publishing process, use it to sell and market your book, and most importantly use it to promote yourself. Social media has become the new town square so get out there and share your work.

I taught myself the writing process and what the internet was able to do for me was to help me develop my writing skills even more. There are endless resources on the internet regarding the writing process, editing, self-publishing, and marketing. There is no middle man, and what the internet does is empower those with a dream, those who dream to be a self-published author or anything else in life. It's an amazing tool to have in this period in time. Humanity now has the ability to educate, develop, create, and turn their art into something successful. As an independent author you should utilize all the internet has to offer, there are no excuses.

<u>26</u>

No matter how you feel at the moment, channel those emotions into your writing.

Some of the best writing comes from pure emotions. Let it flow out as you would when you want to tell the person you love that you love them, or release the rage brewing within onto the pages as you would with explicit words. It doesn't matter how good or bad you feel within what matters is how truthful the words that come out are and how effective they become.

As humans we feel an array of emotions throughout a single day and when someone can feel what you are feeling by just reading your words that is powerful, that is the magic of writing. Anything less of writing with pure emotion may seem mundane. You'll lose your readers.

Do not be afraid to let it all out and dive into the deepest parts of your heart and soul. Release all that comes from within and leave nothing bottled up. The release will feel refreshing and will bring life to your writing.

<u>27</u>

Write what feels right.

Always write what feels right no matter how strange or controversial it may seem to be. The feelings from within will always guide you and lead you into the right direction. Never be afraid because if what you write seems right no matter what the outcome is there will be no regret.

At times it can be difficult to write what feels right within because of the fear of what others may think or what may become of the story or character. Go with it no matter what because in the end if the choice of words was right then you have no worries and if they are the wrong words then you will be able to learn from your mistake, carry on and write something even better. Writing what feels right is always the truth that shines light.

<u>28</u>

Foolishly go with the flow of life, no matter what they say you will always get there your way.

It is the fool that strolls along with his head in the air for there is unlimited potential that awaits him. Live life like a child who blindly sets out into the unknown unafraid yet filled with curiosity for all that awaits him at the end of the journey. Having this carefree way of living is essential with writing, because it is this way of being which brings out the magic in writing.

The imagination is fueled with foolish thinking and ways of life. Channel this foolish energy and flow with it. Foolishly write and go with what flows from the heart. The innocence from within is sometimes the fire needed to get you where you want, so foolishly live life and write what feels right.

<u>29</u>

Try not to submit to writing just one genre, instead commit to writing many genres, you'll become a well-rounded and valuable writer.

As a writer be as diverse as you can be. Never limit yourself to one genre. Write to tell stories not to fit into a peg hole. Know that there are many avid readers out there, many of whom enjoy many different genres. So instead of writing for a limited audience write for a wider array of readers.

It's refreshing and always challenging as a writer to write differently each time. There is growth with writing many different genres and it's rewarding. It is also more fun. Think about how you would feel if you were to read the same genre over, and over again. It gets boring, as does it with writing.

<u>30</u>

Write without fear of what others will think. The only opinion that matters is your own.

The greatest fear in life is the fear of worrying about what other people think. Get out of this prison and write freely. You will limit yourself as a writer if every time you hold yourself back from writing what's on your mind because of what this person, or that person may think. Fuck em' and just write what's in your heart. No matter if it is right or wrong it will always be your truth.

Remember write for you and no one else. In the end no matter what critiques or advice you get it is your opinion that matters most. So write on and go with it. Even if the masses may feel offended or dislike what you write, that's ok, because you may be able to inspire one person and help them with their life. That is what writing is all about, making that soul connection with the reader, making them feel something and giving them some sort of inspiration and hope.

<u>31</u>

The first and the last word of a book will be the hardest words to write.

These are the hardest words to write because the first word is like taking your first step down a new path and the last word is that final step you take when you get to your destination. The first word sets the tone of the whole story; it is the seed which begins to grow into a beautiful tree. That final word is the top, the crown of everything that has been created and written.

The amount and time and effort you put into writing a book can become overshadowed by the first and last word for better or for worse. People will always read the first word before reading a book and always skip all pages and curiously look at the end of a book if they are considering reading it. Try to grasp their attention with just one word and keep them wanting to read more.

<u>32</u>

Your first book will be the hardest book to write and will take the longest time to complete.

It took me 10 years to write my first novel Esperanza. For others their first book may take half the time it took me or less. Either way, no matter who you are that first book you write, will take the longest, because there is a whole process that needs to be mastered. Not only is writing your first book difficult regarding the content, but it is a learning experience as well. There is so much to the writing process that needs to be implemented into writing, some of which cannot be taught but learnt from experience.

Everyone is different and the process is not the same for everyone. As you write your first book you will start to learn and understand this. When you do then you will discover what works for you. That is the beauty of writing your first book because in the end after it is published, when you set out to write another book the process will be so much smoother and it won't take as long as it took to write as your first book.

33

If you want to become a full-time writer you must treat the process like your job. You need to be discipline and have good time management.

This is the reality, as with anything in life you want to pursue and do full-time you have to put in the work, and you have to want to love the process. If being a full-time writer is your desire then sitting around day after day sulking or not putting in quality time and effort into writing isn't going to get you to where you want to be.

There is no wrong or right way of achieving the dream of living life as a full-time writer, it can be done, but it is all up to your perspective. How bad do you want it? So if you are working your day job for 8 hours a day, then you need to find a way to write for at least 2-4 hours a day. If this seems impossible then maybe writing isn't for you. The reality is there are 24 hours in a day so there are no excuses for not finding the time. Even if you have to divide that time up by writing for 1 hour in the morning, 1 hour in the afternoon, 20-30 minutes after your day job and then for another 1 hour before bed time. However you live your life, especially with how you need to find a way to get the job done at work, then you can find a way to write in order to become a full-time writer.

<u>34</u>

Never compare yourself to other writers.

This is something all humans do, we compare ourselves to others. At times it can be fun to flirt with the idea of being just as good of a writer as a New York Times best-selling author but at the same time it can become depressing to think that you can never amount to someone of that stature.

This is why you should never compare yourself to other writers. All writers are different. Be you, be your own entity and be unique. Stop worrying about other writers, what they are writing, how successful they are or how many books they have written. They aren't you and you aren't them. We seem to live in a time when people are obsessed with worrying and wondering about what other people are doing and wanting to emulate them. Social media plays a factor in this. Don't get sucked into the negative dogma of comparing yourself to others because it will do nothing but hold you back from your true potential.

35

Be authentic with your writing.

Be truthful to yourself and with all you write and people will have more respect for you as a writer. Don't try to write like other writers or write in a way that best suites an audience. Use your voice; be unique and different from the rest. That's what writing is all about; it's about discovering your inner voice and sharing it with the world.

There is always a yearning for something different within all of us. So be the writer that writes something different, be the writer that is original and be the writer that stays away from the crowd and stands out. Do not be afraid to write with the truth from within because you never know that authentic voice that you share may shed some light on someone who seeks some hope and inspiration. Be the voice that enlightens and uplifts someone's heart and soul.

<u>36</u>

Have vision; foresee the ultimate outcome you want before finishing your book. By doing this the process will flow smoother, it will inspire you, and drive you to finish your book.

Every dream you imagine achieving in life should be monumental. The bigger the dream the more hungry you should become. No matter how ridiculously big the dream may be, dream it, and fantasize with the idea of achieving that dream. This will fuel your heart and soul, but at the same time you need to be grounded with the process and the steps taken to achieve all the little goals and paths needed to be conquered along the way.

Having vision and foreseeing the unknown road which lies ahead will better prepare you for this journey. Others may have taken roads similar to the one you venture down, so learn from them and find your own way with mapping out the course you want to take. The writing will flow out and the book you dream to write will eventually become a reality.

<u>37</u>

Be open minded with the many paths your characters could take, there are no wrong ways to go.

As with life so will your characters have many different life paths and choices to make. There is no wrong or right way for them, so don't be afraid to play around with all the different paths a character can take. No matter how strange, crazy, or outlandish a choice or path a character can take is, try it and go with it. Some of the most memorable scenes in stories are when characters take the least likely path.

Have fun with this part of the writing and play around with it. Enjoy this process. A lot of times this part of the writing can help better develop your character or even help with molding the plot into something different and or better. This is what makes writing fun and enjoyable.

<u>38</u>

Dream like a child dreams and write with the heart of a child.

Sometimes you have to unleash the inner child when writing. The innocence from within, that child should never fade away. There is something magical about a child's imagination, so to dream like a child and write with the curiosity of a child is powerful. Tap into this innocent energy and channel it into your writing.

Dreams are what make us believe so believe that you can write a magical story. Believe like a child believes in magic, dragons, and fairies. Never grow old, stay forever young with the way you live your life and the way you write.

39

Never lose the curiosity of a child, question everything and go with the most bizarre characters and scenarios you may imagine.

Wonder and ask questions like a child. Have a sense of awe for the universe and the unknown the way a child would. It are these questions we ask ourselves regarding our characters and story we are writing which will open up doors. As with all children who question so should you and never feel that something you imagined is too bizarre or unrealistic to write. Nothing is impossible or strange in the eyes of a child, everything is interesting.

Learn from questions as would a child and imagine how you can write something for the better. Never limit yourself and always look up to the stars, and write with wonder and awe. Children sometimes open up our eyes to see the beauty within all so do not be afraid to question all you have done and then transform it into the unimaginable. Curiosity and imagination are keys to unlocking the universe within.

<u>40</u>
Don't be afraid to be you.

There is only one you in this world so be you. Don't worry about others and what they think. The opinions of others do not define you so tap into your heart and soul and discover who you are. Share your uniqueness with the world and open up doors in the hearts and minds of others with all you behold. This is the beauty of being you.

So inspire others with your words and be the light that guides those trying to discover their own paths in life. Yours could be the one that paves the way for others. You can be the voice that creates change and oneness. You can be the one that writes something special for all to love.

<u>41</u>

Keep your characters and story universal.

No matter what kind of character or story you create always try to find a way to make them universal so that people from all walks of life will be able to connect. Stories are what drive the human spirit and characters are what motivate and inspire people. By creating something universal you won't limit the possibilities of connecting with a mass of people from around the world.

Ultimately as writers this is what we strive to do, to write a story that people from all over the world can enjoy. Making the characters and story universal will enable this possibility. Do not stress over this idea though, rather search for a character and story that all people can relate to, something that taps into the emotions that all humans experience no matter how old, where you are from or what ethnicity you are. Creating an emotional driving force is what will help with writing something universal.

42

Never allow your ideas to fade away. Water them every now and again and they will grow into something special.

It doesn't matter what kind of idea it is, all ideas have the possibility of growth. Ideas are seeds, waiting to grow into a strong tree. So whatever ideas come into your mind that is something you want to pursue or has potential, go with. You never know what it may grow into.

Also know that all ideas are gems buried deep within the mind. Find them and unleash them. Ideas have value, and some ideas are worth stealing. So protecting your ideas is just as important as watering them. Be careful who you share your ideas with; yet open up about all that you envision. Bring an idea to life, nourish it and protect it so that when it grows you have golden apples to pick from your tree of ideas.

<u>43</u>

Life experiences are great to write about, but always add a bit of your imagination to make it magical.

As with food adding a little spice to life makes it a bit better. Think about all the times you tell a story to a friend, co-worker or family member, it usually isn't exactly the way it happened, we always tend to add in a little bit more to make it better. This is the same with writing a story; in order to keep a reader more engaged it's best to add more imagination.

This is where the magic comes from, that little bit of extra sauce of words to spice things up. No matter if the story you are telling is based off of a real person or events or if it is fictional the more imagination and spicier it is the more people will want to read. Stay away from bland writing and spice it up, use your imagination and make magic.

<u>44</u>

There is magic in words.

Words are like spells that can take control of your emotions. They can take us away to a better place or someplace surreal or not of this world. Words can inspire us and motivate us. They could also cut us and tear us a part, but could heal wounds and mend together all the broken pieces.

Words can open up doors of possibilities and take us beyond all that is impossible. Words can be the light that fills a darken room. Words can guide us and mislead us, but could also open our eyes so that we can see what is right and what is wrong. Words are the truth from which we hide and the lies we keep by our side. They are the gatekeepers to the mind and the rivers that flow across pages. Words can erase all of time and can bring us back to a safer place in time. Words are what make dreams come alive.

<u>45</u>

Never allow the systematic daily routines of life to take control of you; your ideas and writing will die with you.

Life isn't easy, it was never meant to be. We are consciousness having an experience on Earth and being tested daily. The systematic daily routines of life can be overwhelming at times as can internal and external conflicts. No matter what barriers come your way, disputes, or chains of life get shackled onto you, never allow all the negativity to consume you and kill all you behold inside.

Our life can change at any given moment for better or for worse, so be prepared to protect your ideas and find a way to continue writing. Not only is life a gift but so are the ideas we hold within; don't allow them to fade away don't allow the way the world is to keep you from writing. Find a way to heal and make it work. Don't allow it to die with you as you push your way through the systematic daily routines. Find peace within, find a way to balance and write, bring life.

<u>46</u>

It's ok to feel alone and sad, some of the best writing comes from these
emotions.

Loneliness isn't a disease it's an escape from the mad world we live in.
Yes there are people out there who are lonely because they cannot find the right
person or group to be with, and there are those who feel sad because of this. It's
ok the universe has a master plan for all.

Instead of loathing and sulking with loneliness and sadness; embrace it.
Embrace those forgotten and disliked emotions; channel the feelings from within
into words. Write these feelings for they are just as meaningful as words of
happiness.

<u>47</u>

Write with an open mind.

An open mind creates an ocean of possibilities. There are infinite pathways and doors waiting to be taken and opened. For a writer this is where you want to be freely swimming, dreaming and utilizing the limitless droplets of water filled with ideas, inspiration and imagination.

A closed mind can be like a prison, it can hold you back, keep you living a mundane life, without understanding and being judgmental without knowing. This is not the way of a writer, a writer needs to be free to express themselves and write about anything without worrying about critical closed minds that cannot see all that a writer sees.

<u>48</u>

No matter how long a project takes, never let it die; stick with it until the end.

Always finish what you started. This should be a virtue all writers abide by. Do not allow the duration of time to hold you back, divert you or be the reason to abandon and abort a writing project. All things of worth take time to create.

This is so with writing a book. It takes time, lots of time. So many people talk about writing a book but not many are willing to put in the amount of time and effort it takes to write and finish a book. Patience is key and vital. Without it you'll fail and let a project die before ever knowing what its worth. Treat a writing project as you would a seed; water it, nourish and take care of it until it is fully grown. Bring life not death so that all that you create brings light to someone who is seeking a beacon of hope.

<u>49</u>

The sun and the moon will always rise and fall as will you with writing.

The sun and the moon rising and falling along with emotions is part of the cycle of life. The same is true with writing. There will be good days and there will be bad days. This is expected and it is something to not be afraid of. Know that when there is darkness light is sure to come. Yes, it sucks having a bad writing day, those days when there is nothing to write, you can't focus or think and you can end up staring at a blank piece of paper for hours. Even more horrific is not being able to write for days.

It's ok; those periods of writer's block will come and go. They will fade away and when you least expect it brighter days will bring sparks of inspiration. Take advantage of the sunny days and write like there is no tomorrow so that when the storm clouds come you won't feel as if you have fallen behind that much when there is no writing happening. Embrace the light and the dark, except the days when you can write and cannot for there is a universal cycle that we all live by, a cycle we learn from, adapt to and write with.

<u>50</u>

Conquer each day as if it's your last.

This is a healthy approach to life for all. Live life to the fullest, don't live with regrets. This is true for writers. As writers we must write each day as if it is our last, or at least attempt to. Writing with this mentality will up your writing game; it will challenge you and push you to write more each day than before. Knowing that you are going to die will encourage you to write each day as if it is your last. To not leave any unfinished work behind should be a form of motivation.

Think about it. Think about all the ideas, outlines, and projects on the shelf that if you were to die today all those beautiful seeds would die with you. Don't allow this to happen by not taking advantage of each day. Write. Write like there is no tomorrow, even if you only write a word a day, make it meaningful. Write for today because tomorrow may never come.

<u>51</u>

Each page is a fresh new beginning.

No matter what was written in the past every blank page is a canvas waiting to be manifested into something new. This is the beauty of every new page. You get to start fresh, carry on from where you left off or left behind. It's an opportunity to write something new. It's the space to build off of the recent page. Even if you have an idea or the direction you want to go, the blank page is still filled with endless possibilities.

As stressful as it can be at times to stare at a blank page pondering what to write, know that once you start putting words onto the page magic will begin to happen. Forget about the past and focus on the moment you begin writing on a new page because it is here where something new begins to take form and mold into something beautiful. It is here where new beginnings begin.

<u>52</u>

Writing is an art that takes time to master; have patience.

As with anything in life time is essential when it comes to mastering a craft. Writing is no different. No matter how established you are, or how amateur you are the development process should never end. This is part of mastery, to write with a growth mindset, to always strive to be better than before.

Mastery takes time though and it isn't easy. To master a craft isn't a path many are willing to take. It's a long treacherous road many may consider taking but once the reality of how difficult and long it will take it will most likely be abandoned. Patience is key since in order for one to develop and master the art of writing you must be willing to stay on the long road. It can bring burden, break up relationships, and bring internal and external stress but know that if you are willing and able to conquer all that tries to hold you back or stop you there is an ocean of possibilities and internal and external triumphs that await you.

<u>53</u>

Before writing a book make sure to look at what lies ahead; the road isn't
straight, nor is it short and bright.

It's a treacherous path, it's dark and filled with trenches, pain, agony, and
burden and that's just the beginning before you get to the many mountain ranges
that await you. If you are willing to take the task and stay strong then good luck
to you my friend, for I'll see you somewhere near the end.

This is the reality of writing a book. It isn't like taking a Sunday stroll
through the park on a warm sunny day. It isn't cool and sexy. It can be more like
storming the beaches of Iwo-Jima during WWII, where at any moment there is
disaster or death awaiting you and your book. Yes, many people have the
thought or say that "I can write a book about that or this," but what most people
don't realize is how fucking difficult it is. Yes you can probably hack out a book
in a month or two, but what about the quality of it. Or you can spend years
writing a book, but for what purpose. These are just some of the many avenues
that await aspiring writers and what I can say no matter what kind of book you
want to write be ready to be faced with multiple internal and external barriers,
but if you have the will power, the patience and the hunger to take such a
strenuous path I wish you the best of luck and support you, just once you take
that first step never stop until you get to the end. Leave nothing unfinished
always complete what you started.

<u>54</u>

Find some inspiration, something to keep you motivated.

We all need a little inspiration in our lives, something to motivate and get us moving. Whoever it is or whatever it is that inspires you utilize the feeling that it gives you, go with it, and channel it into your writing. Whether it's a great writer, artist, film director, historical figure, public figure, someone famous, a parent, a sibling, a friend, a teacher, a coach or just some stranger in a café, if someone inspires you they should always be the one you go to or think of when times get tough or you feel down.

It doesn't even have to be a person; it could be a beautiful piece of art, a book, a movie, a park, nature, an animal, an event, a public place, or the cosmos that brings you a sense of inspiration. Inspiration is magical; it can transform someone and fuel them to do great things with their lives. Be inspired to write, write to inspire others.

<u>55</u>

Having a muse to frequently ponder helps with the writing, your heart will spill words out onto the pages.

Muses can be like angels, supernatural beings sent to heal the heart and soul. In the eyes of an artist muses can be idols put on top of a pedestal. This may upset a spouse or a loved one but I assure you that all thoughts and intentions are for innocent inspiration. It may be difficult to comprehend for some but an artist, a writer or someone seeking spiritual inspiration a muse is the closest entity to cosmic enlightment, an energy source not of this world which can fuel the heart and soul.

This is why muses are sought by the creative mind. There is a bond which is like no other, something magical; something that cannot be explained. Their unworldly qualities and way of being can spark a fire deep inside. Having a muse to ponder unleashes the creative lion which slumbers deep within.

<u>56</u>

Write for no one, yet write for something.

This has to do with being authentic as a writer. Yes we want to hit a target audience, but at what cost. Are you willing to be unauthentic and write without deeper meaning? That is why it is more powerful to write for something rather than for someone.

Write from within; write what you feel from your heart and soul about something you believe in. This could be anything so long as it has a message to be taught or learned. You will also limit yourself from your true potential if you focus on a certain group or trend. Try to stay away from the crowd, write what feels right; write for something.

<u>57</u>

Use your emotions to fuel your writing.

Don't be afraid to unleash your emotions onto the blank pages. No matter what you feel within go with it and channel it into your writing. Take advantage of the moment; use your emotions to add layers and authenticity to all that you write. If you're feeling sad write and create a mellow mood. If you are feeling happy write and create a sense of joy.

All that you write should change like the tides; they should contrast yet mend together in perfect harmony. As with the different emotions you feel throughout the day so should all that you write change and have a balance. Drive your story forward with pure emotions and grasp your reader with all that you feel, take them along for the ride and give them an emotional experience like never before.

<u>58</u>

It should take about one season to complete an average size book.

If you stick with a writing schedule and follow through it should take about 3 to 4 months to complete an average size book of about 300 pages. Will this be the final cut which is ready for publication; absolutely not. No way, what it will be though is a first draft, the blue prints you will then take to mold into a final draft.

Discipline is vital if you want to complete a book in one season. Time management and work ethic will play a big factor in completing a book in such a seasonal amount of time. One strategy to use is to try and complete 100 pages in a month. Think about it, if a month has 30 days and you average 4 pages a day then this goal of writing 100 pages in a month can be reached and if you stick with it 300 pages can be completed in one season. Ultimately what it comes down to is the process and how you go about it, and whatever your process is know that writing a book in one season can be done even by an amateur writer.

<u>59</u>

Write with the mood of the seasons.

Depending on the book you are writing sometimes it is a good idea to write with the mood of a season. If you are writing something dark, scary, or suspenseful maybe writing during the long dark cold days of winter would be a good time to write such a story. If you plan on writing something more upbeat then maybe the long warm days of summer would be a good time to write.

This is all up to the individual. Everyone is different and feel differently during each season. Some may enjoy the long, dark cold winter months and dislike the warm sunny summer days, while others will dislike the winter and love summer. That is ok, just go with the mood the season brings and write.

<u>60</u>

Ideas come randomly like leaves falling from trees. Be sure to recognize each idea and pick it up. It may be worth more than you think.

Never leave an idea untouched. Grasp it and keep it. Even if you don't use it at the moment, save it for another time, for it may be of worth later in time. Yes not every idea will be a good one, but nourish it and try to turn it into gold.

Never walk by the ideas that drop before your eyes, they come for reasons unknown; it's up to you to figure out why. The random ideas that come and go have deeper meaning, they can be the answer you've been looking for. So never let them fade away, and never leave it on the ground because one day it will blossom into a beautiful tree and the book that you write will fill others with ideas and inspiration.

61

Writers telling the truth are dangerous during times of universal deceit.

Presently writers who speak truth have either been shadow banned, censored, black listed, completely removed from social media platforms, arrested, living in exile, or killed off. This is the truth and this is the truth about how powerful a writer's voice can be. As we live through one of the most defining times in human history what is truth is constantly being used as a weapon to enlighten, deceive, or control. The truth has become so twisted and mutated that the real truth sometimes is never known or accepted by the average person. When the real truth is exposed and delivered the writers who are bold enough to do so usually become the victims.

That's why it is so important as of now for writers to rise up and write the truth. Whatever that truth may be, unleash it and let it spread like a wildfire. Open up the minds of the blind and corrupted and set them free. Do not be afraid to write the truth.

62

The pen is a writer's weapon.

Such a small piece of plastic filled with ink is more powerful than a gun. The laws that control and dictate a nation are signed with a pen and easily like that freedoms can be taken away, regulations can be made and the leaders of nations can change the whole fabric of society with the stroke of a pen.

This is so for a writer with an idea. A writer who can use his weapon for good, and unleash his full magazine of imagination onto the pages he writes can create a social wave of truth and freedom. Know that the pen you use is more powerful than any standing army; that ideas can bring down walls, and ideas can change the whole paradigm of the masses. Never take for granted how powerful the pen can be when in the hands of a writer.

63

Words

Words can inspire, words can deceive, words can control, words can divide, words can unite, words can give hope, words can bring love, words can bring hate, words can create a movement, words can shut down systematic institutions, words can destroy a character, words can create idols, words can bring peace, words can educate, words can bring laughter, words can motivate, words can open up the mind, words can take away time, words can take you there, words can change the world . . . words are powerful, choose them wisely.

64

Writers are revolutionaries with a pen.

Writers have the ability to create change, defy social injustices, inspire, motivate, uplift the heart and soul, and create an internal and external revolution. Freedom of expression is what every writer lives by and what every writer shares. A writer's thoughts and opinions can shake up the masses and bring down walls. Ideas can be used like bombs and blow up the minds of the people, fill them with reason and create purpose.

A true writer will not bow down to the confines of life nor write within the lines of conformity. A true writer will write truth without regret, and never allow censorship to stop them from creating. Intimidation will not hold a writer with true convictions back nor stop them from freeing minds, a true writer will die writing what's on their mind, a writer will create a revolution with words to better mankind.

<u>65</u>

The art of storytelling will never die, but writers will die out and change. Every generation of writers needs to reinvent the way stories are written and told.

Storytelling is ingrained in the DNA of human beings. It's as tribal as our ancestors and is a part of us that will never die. The platform at which a story is told will change as will the way a story is told; we have seen this throughout the ages. This is inevitable and it's up to writers to find new and inventive ways of writing a story.

Writing has evolved as have writers and so should the way a story is written and told. There is no right or wrong way to write a story, it's about the presentation. How effective is the story and its flow. This is what writers need to mold into something new, the chemistry of a story, the elements that make it alive. Like a magician a writer needs to not only create something from nothing but redefine the way a story is told.

<u>66</u>

There is an infinite amount of stories which can be created and told, do not hold back on a story you have held inside you.

Out of the billions of stories which exist do not allow one brewing in your mind to never have the opportunity to manifest. Yours could be the one that millions of people enjoy. Yours could be the story that inspires or motivates. Yours could be the story that beings someone a sense of peace during chaotic times. Yours could be the one that freezes all of time and takes someone away to a better place.

Know that your story is just as special as the billions of stories that exist. Bring it to life and let it spread its wings, you never know where it will fly to and what it will bring you back. Anything created from the infinite is of worth as are you. Like stardust in the cosmos so is the story you have in you waiting to fly amongst the stars.

<u>67</u>

Don't be intimidated by all the books you see in a book store or a library. Bring your book to life for it may be the one people want to take off the shelf to read.

Seeing so many books on the bookshelves in book stores and in libraries should not bring fear but motivation. You should be hungry to get your book up on the labyrinth of bookshelves with all the other books. As an aspiring writer to walk around the maze of books in book stores and libraries should fill you with a fire that fuels your writing. Wanting to have your book being published and put on a shelf for others to take should be a visual goal all writers have.

Visualize this every day, foresee your book on the best seller's bookshelf or on the employee's favorite shelf. Bring your book to life for others to see. A book store bookshelf is where all writer's dream of having their book, so don't allow the fear of seeing so many books hold you back from completing yours and having it put on the shelves with so many other books.

<u>68</u>

Have persistence, the journey isn't easy nor is it short.

Know that the journey of writing and publishing a book isn't easy nor is it a short one. Writing a book is something that seems sexy and fun but the truth is that it is a long grueling quest that many are not willing to take. If you are bold enough to begin the journey persistence is key to completing such an enriching feat. There will be many barriers and mountains to climb along the way, a lot of heartache and pain. The road will constantly change and sometimes take you back, but no matter how dark or hard it gets if writing a book is your true desire then you need to find the strength within your heart and soul to never give up.

Persistence is the formula needed, and it will get you there. This is the cure to failure and this is the wind behind your back. The moment you give up there will be two deaths, you will carry the burden of for the rest of your life, the death of a story idea and the death of taking action and not finishing what you started; regret. Persistence is what is needed to conquer both internal and external barriers, and persistence is what will get you to your dream of writing and publishing a book.

<u>69</u>

The quality of your work is worth more than the quantity of pages you write.

Dr. Suess' books are a perfect example of how the quality of a book is worth more than the quantity of the pages. These children's books are short in length and the word count is small. Yet, they are extremely powerful stories. They give a universal message to all; the words are monumental yet the books are so small. It's the message, not the size that matters more, and so should the story you dream to write.

As a writer this could be difficult at times because there is so much that we want to say. That is ok, it's after writing the first draft that the quality and the quantity of the book needs to be examined and taken care of. It could be a difficult feat but try to keep your story as simple and universal as possible. Try to avoid the over use of certain words or unnecessary words. Write with the goal to write more will little, and the want to create something of worth for all to remember.

<u>70</u>

Travel often, magical things happen when you're on the road; when the body is in motion ideas pour in from the higher realms of consciousness.

The world is an open book so try to read as many pages are you can. Get out there and experience life, travel to faraway places and explore the unknown. Do not be afraid to meet new and interesting people from all walks of life. Embrace the diversity you find all around and look at the world with a different lens. You'll be surprised at the magic that comes from beyond all that you know.

Think about the feeling you get when traveling, even that excitement felt when packing and getting ready to go. There is something magical about the journey, traveling to some destination no matter how far. The mind begins to open up like never before and ideas seem to magically flow in from nowhere. Take advantage of the time spent on the open road and never let an idea fade away or go unnoticed. Look to travel often and love the journey for it's when the journey is over and we return home that we reminisce about all the amazing places and faces we've seen, and truly appreciate the magical feeling we felt when on the open road.

<u>71</u>

Putting yourself into a meditative state opens up the mind; it enables you to access the universal consciousness. This oneness with the web of consciousness opens up the heart and eyes, ideas will flow and words will be written with swift ease.

Meditation should be part of our everyday lives. It doesn't matter the method at which you meditate, but more about doing it. Even if just for ten minutes a day, find the time to open up your mind, relax the body, and clear your head of toxic thoughts. Allow the beauty of meditation to take hold of you and fill you with positive energy and elaborate ideas.

Magic happens when in a meditative state of being. Make that soul connection with the universe and allow the free flow of the universal consciousness to pour into your mind. For any aspiring writer this should be a part of your down time or method of taking a break from writing. As writers our minds could become flooded with ideas, characters, scenes, scenarios, plot, and all the chaos of dealing with editing and rewrites. Let it all go and spend some time each day to meditate to forget about it all and let new, healthy, and abundant ideas flow in. Take the time to heal from within.

<u>72</u>

Words can hurt. Do not allow negative reviews to bring you down, keep writing no matter what they say.

Words can cut through someone like sharp knives or pierce through the flesh like bullets. As a writer after finally getting your book published part of the marketing all writers must partake in, in order to get some exposure and create some legitimate buzz about your book is to get a book review. Understand that not every book review will be positive and yes someone's opinion can sway the choices avid readers will make when deciding whether or not they want to read your book. When you do receive a negative review as much as it can hurt and suck, do not allow the opinion of one critic to bring you down.

The opinions of others should not dictate how you write, or the process at which you write, nor should it stop you from writing. If anything it should fuel your fire and motivate you to keep writing, and write better than you did before. So instead of sulking because of a negative review, embrace it, learn from it and carry on. Keep writing and keep seeking reviews from other critics. One or many negative reviews should not be the cause of your demise but be the key to open up new doors and inspire you to not only keep writing but to prove them all wrong. So write, and write, and write no matter what they say.

<u>73</u>

Write with the heart and imagination of a child.

As we grow old we should never allow our inner child to ever fade away and die. Nourish the child within, and embrace it. Never allow Neverland to disappear from within us, because that is the magical place to always go to, to get away, to find a sense of peace, and to go to, to find the magic needed to write. Having that imagination of a child is powerful. Children have the ability to bring joy to life and the chaotic world around, there are no boundaries or limits, there is nothing too strange, or odd, and anything is possible. This is the mindset and the attitude a writer needs.

A writer's imagination is precious and so by tapping into that inner child and imagining like a child it can become something valuable, something of worth, something that can open your mind and set you free to write without fear. Children can be fearless and to write with the heart and imagination of a child can be the magic all writers seek.

<u>74</u>

Always look up to the stars with awe. There is something magical about the cosmos, to look up at the night sky with the curiosity of a child and wonder; this is a spiritual connection which can influence your writing in magical ways.

If you can't look up at the cosmos in awe, then you haven't a soul. The vastness of space should always bring a sense of wonder and admiration. Like a child wishes upon a star and gazes up at the night sky wondering if we are alone in the universe, so should a writer look up at the beauty of it all and imagine. Make that spiritual connection with the billions, and billions of stars that fill the night sky. The feeling it brings cannot be explained but it should inspire you to write.

Anything which is as beautiful and mysterious as the cosmos should never be ignored and should be appreciated. For it is something which only muses can be compared to, so take the time to admire its beauty and imagine. Somewhere amongst the stars is an idea waiting to be discovered and brought down to Earth, waiting to be written into a book.

<u>75</u>

Always be authentic to yourself; never worry about what other writers do. Write your own path and others will follow.

As a writer you should seek to discover your own voice and not worry about the voice of other writers. Don't even worry about what they are writing. Write what you feel in your heart, and be authentic. The road of truth may be vast and lonely, but eventually others will discover your truth, appreciate it and follow down the path that you paved.

Be a pioneer and not a follower. Write for you and no one else. You shouldn't have to rely on the opinions of others or worry about the in crowd and what is trendy. This will bog down your writing and hold you back. Take the leap and go your own way, write what feels right within and never hold back what's in your heart.

<u>76</u>

I paint pictures with words.

You need to capture the images in your mind and paint them onto the pages. Your words should be like paint and the pen you write with should be like a paint brush which swiftly paints the image in your mind with big swift brush strokes onto the pages.

If this is executed right your words should come alive and paint a picture in the mind of your reader. This is the magic a writer can create on the pages of their book. So visualize all that you image and use your words to paint a picture for all to see.

<u>77</u>

Visualize the story you are writing in the eye of your mind like a movie on the big screen.

Everything that is written I visualize in my mind. This is a method that works and helps with creating a character, and a scene. To visualize everything like a movie makes the writing flow and come alive. If this is transferred onto the pages affectively the readers should be able to visualize the movie you created in your mind as well.

Movies are the highest art form and to be able to transfer the movie you see in your mind onto the pages for all to see is magical. This is what all writers strive to do, to show a story and have a reader so engaged, and stimulated by the visual imagery they have created in their mind from your words that the reader never wants to put the book down.

<u>78</u>

Writers are like spies in a café; listening to every conversation and observing every patron that walks in.

As a writer this is a moonlighting role which is an effective one to step into. Sometimes it happens by accident. Some of the best story ideas come from life and as a writer who sits in a café often many side conversations can be overheard which have potential to be transformed into a great story. Some of them are humorous, some are disgusting, some are bizarre, some are evil and sometimes they can be inspiring. It can be fun to listen to some of these conversations but at the same time rewarding.

Story ideas and characters can be developed from just one conversation being overheard or from someone who crosses paths with you. People from all walks of life are characters waiting to be born onto blank pages. So like a spy sometimes you have to observe strangers without being rude or being caught. Take notes on their appearance, actions, and the way they speak. Yes this could sound creepy but in the eyes of an artist, especially a writer, strangers are just subjects of a potential piece of work. Do not let a stranger of interest walk away without getting an image of them implanted in your mind, or a good conversation slip by without taking notes. There is an ocean of characters and story ideas floating around in cafes and public spaces so the next time you are there never be afraid to moonlight as a spy.

<u>79</u>

Free to write, write to be free.

Everyone has the freedom to write, so take advantage of this and write to be free. Tell the stories you have buried deep inside or the ones brewing in your mind. These stories have the potential to bring joy to many and abundance to you. Even if the first book you write doesn't bring you the success needed to live as a full time writer, never stop and keep writing. Eventually you and your stories will be found.

If you want to live freely as a writer bad enough you will stop at nothing to reach this goal. You will keep writing no matter what and make it a lifestyle. Take advantage of the freedom you have to write, especially since we live in a time where you can write whatever you wish, as long as it doesn't promote hate or violence. Writing should bring you a sense of peace and freedom for if you love to write you will feel free whenever you do. Also don't forget that words have power and that your words can set others free. Write, never stop and create the freedom you wish for yourself with your words.

<u>80</u>

You must first have the audacity to write and then you will need to be patient to finish.

If your goal is to write a book you cannot be afraid to start, you must be bold to take that first step. Keep in mind though once that first word is written the journey is not set in stone, the final destination cannot be foreseen, nor timed, so it is essential that you have patience. Patience is what will get you from beginning to end. So no matter how audacious you are to begin, know that it is of no worth if you have no patience to finish what you started.

<u>81</u>

Write from wherever, whenever and for however long you want; that is the beauty of writing.

This should be your motivation to become a full time writer, the idea that a writer has the freedom to write from wherever, whenever and for however long you want. Even if you haven't reached this level of success as a writer, know that this can be created to fit your lifestyle. Yes, it could be difficult and frustrating to try and implement a writing schedule into your daily life, but knowing that there are 24 hours in a day it can be done. That is up to you, and how devoted and dedicated you are to writing and becoming a full time writer.

If you are able to balance your life, work, family and writing then you have won. You will be able to write from wherever, whenever and for however long you want, yes that is all up to you and how you create this schedule for yourself. So, there should be no excuses as to why you cannot write daily, from wherever you are and for however long you want. Break it up if you have to, remember if you love to write you will find a way to do it and create a writer's lifestyle.

<u>82</u>

Anything that can be imagined can be written.

Life and everything we know that has been created from humans was first developed in someone's imagination. A person's imagination is powerful so don't allow all that is created from your imagination to be left unnoticed or fade away. Do not be afraid to bring your imagination to life. Write what is created from your imagination and know that anything can be written. There are no borders or rules when it comes to your imagination.

It was Einstein who stated that "Imagination is more important than knowledge. For knowledge is limited to all we now know and understand, while imagination embraces the entire world, and all there ever will be to know and understand." So don't waste your imagination and use it. Create something bold, create something inspiring, create something different and unique and share your imagination with the world for you never know, your imagination may inspire, and change the world.

<u>83</u>

The right words can change a person's life forever.

Words have power. Your words can change a person's life, so do not be afraid to write. No matter how critical you or others can be of your work, don't allow this to stop you from writing or sharing your work. Even if you are only able to change one person with your words, that is a powerful deed to accomplish.

So write without fear of what others may think. Words that some may dislike may be the words that inspire someone to change their life for the better and create something great. In you is the power to create change, in you are the words that can bring light and hope to someone seeking to get out of the darkness. Be the beacon of hope that someone seeks, so do not be afraid to write what's on your mind, your words may be the right words to change a person's life forever.

<u>84</u>

Words are fuel for the heart, mind and soul.

Not only can your words inspire someone, but others' words can also inspire you to write. The right words can be the fuel for your heart, mind and soul which can get you writing. So every now and then take the time to read. Take the time to listen to others' stories. Take the time to discover something new, for you never know what hidden gems you may find in the words of others.

Find the right words to inspire and motivate you to write. It doesn't matter if they come from some prolific figure, historical figure, a successful writer, or from some unknown person listen to what they have to say, and take in what they have written. As you give your own words so shall you receive words from others to help you strive as a writer.

<u>85</u>

A majority of people say they can or should write a book, but don't. Be the one who actually writes a book.

It's easy to say that you can write a book. We hear this all the time from people who say "I can write a book about that," or "someone can write a book about that." But how many of those people actually do take the leap and write a book? So, why not be the one who actually does write a book. Even if you do not have a clue how to begin, that is ok for you will learn along the way. And in the times that we live with the internet and instant access to information you can teach yourself if you choose to.

There are no limits when it comes to writing a book. So if you are one of the people who does write a book know that you can do it your way. Yes there are certain rules that must be followed regarding structure and formatting, but as far as telling a story there is no right or wrong way of doing it. Just write, and in the end you can fix what needs to be fixed. So if you have an idea you want to turn into a book, do it and don't be afraid to start.

<u>86</u>

The writer's journey is similar to the hero's journey; as a writer make sure you come full circle, there is no book without doing so.

As the hero partakes on the hero's journey and faces many different thresholds, benevolent and malevolent characters, some who help along the way and some who try to stop the hero, as they go from the call, into the depths of the belly of the whale, die either physically, internally or symbolically and then becomes reborn as they come full circle, so will you when you take the writer's journey. It is a long quest many dare not take, but know that if your goal is to write a book and actually finish it, then be ready to take a long journey.

Like a hero you as a writer will be faced with many barriers along the way. There will be times when you will want to quit, give up and go back. There will also be times when people will come into your life who will try to distract you, divert you from your path, or try to stop you. As a writer, like the hero you need to be strong, you need to believe and know that no matter what you will make it to the end and reach your goal.

87

Have pride in what you write.

You should always be proud of what you write for it is yours. Especially if you want people to read what you write, you need to believe in what you write. No one will want to read your work if you are not confident or care much about all that you have written. The love and pride you put into your work will show and others will want read your work.

Think of a great leader, one who leads like a lion, those who fight under this leader will fight with all their heart and soul and die for this person. That is the kind of writer you want to strive to be, a writer that shows so much pride in their work that avid readers will want to read all that you write. They will follow you and your work and believe in you.

<u>88</u>

Never allow the confines of life to hold you back from writing the story you want to write.

Everyone lives a different lifestyle so it is up to you to find balance. If you love to write and your goal is to become a full time successful writer then you must find a way to balance life with your writing. There are 24 hours in a day so there should be no excuses for why you cannot divide your day up with work, family, obligations, free time, sleep and writing; even if you write for just one hour a day that is ok.

Find a way to make it work. All the writing you do doesn't have to be done in one sitting, you can divide it up throughout the day. You can get up early write for a little bit, write in the afternoon during your lunch break, and then later in the evening when all are asleep you can write. However you can fit writing into your daily life is up to you. There is no right or wrong way, it is all about balance and being devoted to writing that you will find a way to make it work.

<u>89</u>

Write for everyone, yet no one.

You should find a way to write so that not only will everyone from all walks of life get something out of all you write, but that you stay true to yourself. Write for what you love and believe in, but find a way to make it universal. Yes this could be difficult at times, but it can be done.

It's up to you how you want to pursue this or who it is you are willing to write for. No matter what works, in the end you want to be authentic. You want to always write for you and all you believe in and love. This isn't being selfish or foolish, but it's being honest, it's being truthful. No matter what story you choose to write know that if you can find a way to write for everyone and write for no one but you then you have mastered the art of writing.

90

Writer's block can be extremely frustrating, carry on because as with all things in life it will pass.

This is the most horrific thing that could happen to a writer, the period of not being able to write anything of worth or anything at all. It fucking sucks. It can be depressing and make you want to give up. The writer's block period that comes can be like a storm, so know that as with a storm, they eventually pass by and the sky opens up and becomes clear. This is so with dealing with and getting past writer's block.

So when the dark clouds come and you have nothing to write, even if you try to beat out a page, go with it. This is usually a good time to sit back and take a break from writing and clear your mind. Rest and maybe try to think about where you are with your writing and what the next step should be. And when all clears away and you are able to focus and write again, you'll be surprised how words will flow out and you will look at all you have done from a different perspective. So when you find yourself stuck with writer's block take advantage of this period and use it to cleanse and open the mind so that you are ready to write more and better than before when the sky clears.

<u>91</u>

Finding your writer's voice takes time; when you do it will sound familiar.

The voice which you start to write with will not be the same that you end up with. It takes time to discover your writer's voice, as does the writing process. It will change during the duration of writing a book and writing many books and other projects. That is ok, as with life we all change. Sometimes you may never find your one voice, because every writing project you write may need to have a different voice.

So do not get discourage over finding your writer's voice. Your voice is your own no matter how different it may seem with each piece of work you write. Own it and be proud of the voice that you write with. Yes, some people may discover their writing voice early; others may find it later on, while some may never discover their writer's voice at all. No matter who you may be know that as long as you keep writing your voice will shine no matter what it is you write. It will be found by others and when you do find your writer's voice it will sound familiar to you for it is yours and no one else's.

92

For me a little side distraction like ambient music or the atmosphere and people in a café can stimulate the mind, it fuels my writing.

This is what I call stimulated concentration, how when the senses are stimulated that they are able to connect with the mind and psyche in a manner that heightens focus and consciousness. There is something magical about this how the exchange of energy is able to create such concentration. How is this so? Well it is partly due to the nature of reality the theory that everything in life is a vibrational frequency.

So if you're on the same wave length as all the material objects around you, the people who are near and the music which is playing then you will consciously and energetically be in sync with all, and sort of get this energetic high. Think about when someone walks into a room they either have good or bad vibes and we can feel this. This is to me how stimulated concentration works, that the good energy all around can create positive energy within and help with concentrating. This may not work for all but for me all the side distractions in a café stimulate me to write, and fuels my heart and soul with a positive energy force which I project onto the pages with words.

<u>93</u>

If a writing session isn't going well, it's ok to step away and live life, you may then discover some inspiration to write.

This will happen often. Do not sulk when it does nor give up on whatever project you are writing. Go with it and step away every now and then. Maybe take a walk, go for a run, read something of interest or listen to some good music. Find something that relaxes you and clears your mind. This is healthy and ok and will help get past those shitty writing sessions.

As with life you will have good days and you will have bad days. It sucks, it happens, but no matter what kind of day you are having it's all about how you handle the day. Are you going to go about the day complaining or doing nothing at all or are you going to embrace it, try to learn from whatever experience you are having during a bad writing session, carry on and turn the day into a productive one no matter if you are able to write or not. Get something out of the bad writing session, even if you step away. Learn from it and grow from it.

94

Your words will never die they will live on forever on the pages you write and in others.

This is the beauty of writing, that even though you will die your words will not and will live on forever. Think about that, your words will become immortal as will you. So no matter what it is you write it will always be there for people to discover and read. Even in death you will be able to make a soul connection with those that read your work. You can inspire, motivate, and create change from the grave.

That is a very magical thing to do, is to leave a part of you for the world. Time will pass but you will be forever the same on pages, yet your words will be able to open up the minds of others to a different place and a different time. Even more powerful is if your words are universal and ageless, that no matter how much time has pass, that they still reign true with the current times and those who read will look on in awe and think what a visionary you were, what a brilliant person. Believe that you are great and your words will bring greatness to a stranger in a later time. In death you will bring life to others.

<u>95</u>

Write not because you have to, but because you want to.

If you aspire to be a writer then writing should not feel like a job, it should feel like love. Be so passionate about writing that you want to write every day because you cannot live without doing so. You should wake up each day wanting to write, itching to get out of your day job to sit down and write. Passion is what you should constantly feel when you are writing or even thinking about writing. Like a muse moves the heart and soul so should writing.

Yes there will be times when you may not be in the mood, or you need to meet some sort of deadline either due to a commission or of personal obligations in which you are dreading the idea of writing, it's ok, that's life, as much as we love to do something there will be days of not wanting to do what we love. Go with it. Take a step back and relax. All relationships have these moments, even the most passionate couples who cannot be separate from each other, whose love out shines all have moments of wanting to be alone. So with writing, love it, own it and write with passion and no matter how the day is going, go with the flow and write because you want to.

<u>96</u>

Devotion, passion, and sacrificing will be vital virtues to possess as a writer.

Love the process. If you aspire to be a successful writer you must possess these qualities in order to turn it into a reality. Nothing is worth pursuing if you are not devoted, passionate, or willing to make the sacrifices needed to get there. This is with anything in life. These are the qualities that separate a true pioneer of their craft from those who think about, or say they can do this or that. Take action and write like there is no tomorrow.

It doesn't matter what kind of writer you are, your background, or even the quality of your writing if you devote your life to writing, write with passion, and make all the necessary sacrifices needed then any dream you set as a writer can be achieved. Nothing is impossible it's all about the mindset you possess and what you have in your heart. Listen to your heart that whispers the path you should take and conquer the emotions which try to hold you back. Use these virtues to get you there.

<u>97</u>

Don't allow stories to die with you, write them and share them with the world
plant them so that they may blossom in others.

Stories are flowers and trees waiting to grow. So water the seeds in your mind, even if you do a little bit at a time its ok, have patience and take the time to complete all the stories you have brewing in your mind. As with words stories will live on forever. Don't allow them to die with you.

Create them and share them with the world. There are billions of people in the world and even if your stories reach only one person, it will be worth the effort. Stories are precious and the art of storytelling is ingrained within us all. Share the stories you behold, open up minds and open up eyes. Inspire, motivate, and bring peace and joy. Implant them in others so that they may grow more and more and spread throughout the world. The world is waiting for your stories to be told so don't be afraid to get them out, and write with the idea that you are going to die someday, that all humans are mortal but stories live on forever, stories are immortal, stories never die.

<u>98</u>

Develop a relationship with your characters; get to know them better than some of your closest friends.

As with the story you are writing the characters will become a part of you. So spend quality time getting to know them. You should know everything about them without thinking twice about it. They should be so developed that when you talk about your character with other people the character will seem like a real person. This is how well you want your character to be established.

Your characters, especially the main character should how a distinct look you can visualize, a history, a past with anecdote stories you can share with others, secrets, a voice and way of speaking that you can act out how they are, and they should even have likes, dislikes, interest, and a daily routine such as a real person. They should be so real in your mind that you will talk about them as if you have spent time with them. Developing a character is one of the fun parts of the writing process so spend efficient time creating a character and make them seem as real as your best friend.

<u>99</u>

Imagine a world like no other and people will come.

The beauty with writing is that anything is possible and any place can be created. There are no rules or regulations, especially when it comes to developing the world you want to write about. It could be based off the real world, a fictional city or town, or it can be an elaborate fantasy world that was created from nothing. Do not be afraid to experiment and create the worlds that develop in your mind, even if you intertwine the real world with fantasy. That is ok. Go with it and create a beautiful and unique place for others.

Even if the world you create is dark and dim, a dystopia no one dares to live within, make it seem so real that people will be transported there when they read. Either way no matter if the world you create is a happy place or a sad place, if you make it feel real then people will surely come.

100
Write, write, write, write, write . . . .

Never stop writing. Write like there is no tomorrow. Get up every day and write. For if writing is your true passion and purpose you should write as if you can't live without doing so. No matter how the world around treats you or the circumstances find the time to write. There's no excuse for not writing each day even if you write just one word bring your thoughts and imagination to life, never let them die.

Writing should be fuel for the heart, mind, and soul. Go about the writing process with this in mind and it will never seem to be too burdensome or a waste of time when there isn't much to say. Write on and live free, let your words set the world free.

<u>101</u>
Never stop writing.

Never stop writing. Never allow the seeds buried deep inside of you to die. Never let a day pass without writing just one word. Never let an idea slip away. Never let your imagination fade away. Never stop writing, even when you have nothing to say. Never allow negative influences or words hold you back. Never allow a single moment to interfere with your journey. Never allow your dreams to disappear. Never ever stop writing.

Part III

Reflections and Inspiration

Revista de Esperanza

~The Beginning~

This isn't an ideal account of an average migrant venturing off into the unknown in search of a better life somewhere over the U.S., Mexico border. I believe that most illegal immigrants crossing over the U.S., Mexico border have moral intentions, in order to escape poverty, a dysfunctional government system, persecution, cross over for personal growth, and, or for their children and family. And yes, there are some bad apples, "some bad hombres," that cross over to escape incarceration and, or prosecution, and end up causing more harm in the United States than good. The political stance revolved around illegal immigration was never my focus or intentions. The idea from the very beginning was to have Dante and Gabriela, literally go through hell.

Although Gabriela is the protagonist in the story, it is Dante and Sarita who were created first. I was going through a transitional period in my life. I just graduated from college, and three years before that, to six months after graduation, (June 2004-June 2007) within that time frame I was rediscovering myself as a person. I went from athlete to artist. Soccer was my primary focus in life from a very young age, until playing and finishing four years of soccer at the college level. Being a part of the 2001 DIII national championship team for The Richard Stockton College of New Jersey was the pinnacle of my soccer career, and that was the beginning of my descent into dark waters, but also when the seeds of living a life as an independent artist were planted.

The character of Dante is somewhat of a shadow self; a persona experiencing the hell I was internally living in. The excessive drinking, the drug use and involvement in a life of crime; those were fictional elements added to the character to create and shadow the hellish state of being I was feeling inside.

Sarita was thrown into the mix as a way of being Dante's savior, the only thing good in his life, who was meant to bring him out of hell. I thought it would be interesting to see how a relationship between a depressed, struggling artist and a young girl who was abandoned and left in his care would be.

And that is how the story of Esperanza began. It was only supposed to be a short story, one of a handful I began writing in early 2007, since I've never written a book before or have ever attempted to. At this time in my live I was playing around with different art mediums; painting, photography, and writing with wanting to eventually get into filmmaking and make movies.(The big picture for me, and still is). Writing seemed to be what I was best at, (Even though my writing was still amateur and needed a lot of work, A LOT).

Gabriela was developed after creating Dante and Sarita. Sarita needed a mother. Who Gabriela was at the time I didn't know. Then it all came to me at once. I was working in a fish market at the time, and during my lunch break and anytime I could find some free time to write, I would. I would write on scraps of paper, napkins, and read the dictionary on my breaks. Co-workers would mock me, and strangers would stare, but I did not care. There were bigger and better things happening inside my mind. I remember while working the fish market counter, taking care of customers, and filleting fish, that I had a sudden thought spark inside my mind. I didn't want to lose it, and kept repeating the thought in my mind until I had my lunch break. That's when I wrote down that Gabriela was an illegal immigrant from Mexico.

Why was Gabriela an illegal immigrant from Mexico? Not only did I work with Latin American immigrants, and knew some illegal ones, but also during this time in life, the illegal immigration debate was hot. It seemed to be on the news 24/7, and I recall Lou Dobbs, and Glenn Beck passionately speaking about the issue a lot. It was echoing in my ear. From that I had the why question on my mind. Why would Gabriela come to America illegally? Obviously to live a better life, but I wanted her path to be dark, and unforgiving; I wanted to throw her into the depths of hell in order to reach her dream. So, I went with having her be associated with a crime syndicate, bringing drugs into the U.S. in order for her to get over the border. Then from that, I decided to have her break away from a life of crime, since she never really wanted any of that. That's why I had her get abducted and then deported back to Mexico. And this is what got me to the beginning, Sarita ending up in the care of Dante. Now what?

(Spoiler Alert) What if Sarita wants to get back to her mother in Mexico, and what if Dante is trying to go to Mexico to get away from his past? That's how the journey cross country began. The focus of the story was on Dante and Sarita, there was really not much thought put into Gabriela, who she is, and her life. And it was as I began writing the first draft that I developed the idea that Sarita is Dante's daughter.

This was supposed to be the big secret the expose at the end of the story. It needed a lot of work to make it convincing. Many drafts were written, many characters added, taken away, and added. More about who Gabriela was and who Dante was, was developed, and then more about the crime syndicate Dante and Gabriela were both a part of. It took me ten years to finally complete Esperanza. The characters and the story have dramatically changed from beginning to end. It evolved, as did I as a person, and a writer.

Metamorphosis

    The Monarch butterfly from the beginning was always meant to be thrown into the story to emulate not only the character of Gabriela, but myself and Latin American migrants. Gabriela more so, since Monarchs which come from Mexico, travel to the far ends of North America, and then return reflects what Gabriela experiences in the story. Dante and Sarita go on their, there and back again journey as well, but ultimately all three characters evolve and change throughout the story. As for me, as mentioned, I was going through a metamorphosis phase in my life as well; changing and growing as a human being, and as a writer.

    Transitioning from a life of soccer to the life of an artist at first was extremely difficult for me. Soccer was my life and a part of my daily routine year after year. When playing soccer at a competitive level ended for me it was devastating. I went through a period of depression since I didn't know what path to take in life. Writing saved me and fueled me to carry on and pursue the life of an independent artist. Writing became my new obsession.

    The transition from athlete to artist wasn't easy. It took a lot of time to adjust and make that life change. So, I used what I knew from soccer, utilized the character traits and actions needed to be successful, and adapted to the life of being a writer.

    Being an independent author was now the new path I ventured down. The unknown trails were dark, treacherous, and mysterious, but I was not afraid. The deeper into the unknown I went, the brighter it became. Little by little I transformed and evolved as a writer. Eventually like a butterfly I grew my wings and flew out into the world, and now fly as a published indie author. Where I go from here I don't know, but wherever the path of an indie author guides me, I know that my heart will take me there.

Stranger than Fiction

The fictional Gabriela was envisioned and created, before I met the real life Gabriela, who is now my wife. Both the REAL LIFE Gabriela and the fictional Gabriela are from Mexico, but they are completely DIFFERENT PEOPLE, who live different lives with different aspirations. My wife is an intelligent, ambitious, beautiful entrepreneur, independent business owner. She is also the jack boot I need to kick me in the ass, and get me moving with life, achieving my goals, and my writing. It is said that behind every successful man, there is a great woman. This I believe, because she is not only my complete opposite, my soulmate, but the logic, and motivation I need to create and be bold with my work and my life; my wife is the weight I need to balance my life.

Our unconventional way of living and love for one another are the roots which hold all together. Gabriela is a motivated woman who is driven to defy all the odds and succeed no matter what. I have so much love and respect for how strong my wife is for being so far away from home and family in Mexico; how she's able to live and continue to chase her dreams from so far away from all she loves.

This journey she took I'm grateful to be a part of. I'm fortunate to have her by my side, even during the darkest of times, as mentioned the jack boot that kicks me in the ass when needed, she gives me reason to live, no matter how hard times can get we pick each other up and carry on the unknown path together without regrets.

Gabriela is my inspiration to become a better man, my biggest critic whose words help to mold me into all that I am possible of becoming. She's my guide and light who walks besides me as I travel through this game called life. She's the warmest, most loving mother, an idol in our daughters' eyes, for she is the image of divinity, a Madonna in the sky, the sacred feminine with angel wings sent to create perfect harmony with all those she loves.

An Aries and a Pisces may not fit together but we found a way to make it work and last no matter what they say, our zodiac signs are strong, mutable and defy all the cosmic laws woven in the stars, for we are not afraid to take risks and chase dreams for this I love my wife and will always respect all that she does, for she's the fiercest angel I've ever known who will love with all her heart and soul and use her fire from within her heart to conquer all the world and all that she seeks.

She's the Temple mount many worshiped who wished that she was still there, but now she's here with me, for that I am thankful. I am fortunate that in my eyes Gabriela found truth and in her eyes I found love. I love the way she is no matter what. I love the way she executes all that she approaches, I love the way she takes on life without fear and I love the way she is.

Gabriela is the strongest woman I've ever known, an angel with the strength of a 1,000 horses chasing dreams, a goddess who rises above all who tries to defy all, a woman of worth, a woman of wit, a woman of style, a woman of grace, a woman of truth, a woman little girls wish to be, a woman who can freeze all of time with the slip of a radiant smile, a woman who swims against the current and finds a way up stream to the infinity pool hidden in the mountain peaks, many dare not try to find, a woman who knows what she wants and isn't swayed by the opinions of others, a woman who can win against all the odds, a woman who I admire and love, a woman I am thankful to have in my life, a woman who will conquer all that she seeks and dreams to be, for this I love you.

Kubrick, Reznor, Rodriguez and Tarantino

These are the independent artists that I am not only a fan of, but who have inspired and influenced me as an independent artist. In the 90's as a tween/teenager I discovered, Stanley Kubrick, Trent Reznor, Robert Rodriguez, and Quentin Tarantino. Nine Inch Nails music was the soundtrack to my life, an alienated adolescent trying to find himself in a world so cruel, while Full Metal Jacket, Desperado and Pulp Fiction were an engaging and entertaining escape from the reality of life, and the harshness of school. I wasn't a Goth, an Emo, a skater, a jock, an estrange artist, a freak, a geek, a nerd, a loser, a Johnny sweatpants, a graphic-T wearing average Joe, the all American blue ribbon scholar, a Rico Suave, or any other typical middle/high school student label; I was a little bit of all. I was a typical awkward teenager, who had friends from all walks of life, and would be welcome at any lunch table, but at this time of my life, I lived in an eggshell; I was extremely quiet and shy. I could be sitting at a table of three and you wouldn't even know I was there.

With Trent Reznor's music I felt alive. No matter how controversial or explicit the lyrics were, the music fueled me, I felt energized. Trent Reznor's music got me through some dark and tough times at that time in my life, and I thank him for that, but most importantly inspiring me as an artist. During the pre-internet era, and being the isolated musician Trent Reznor was during earlier stages in his career, there wasn't much information about his personal life. He had this mystic about him, which I could relate to being the Pisces I am, and when I discovered that he was Nine Inch Nails, that he wrote the lyrics, and most of the music, I admired that. All he did was hire a band to play with him. Knowing that he was the creative force behind Nine Inch Nails, this I loved, and although I was focused on soccer at this time in my life, way back, in the dark corners of my mind, there was an artist screaming to come out, and saying, "That's how I want to do it, I want to be an independent artist like that." I wanted to create my own original pieces of art, and do it my way. What kind of art would I create? Although I didn't have an idea or any ambition at this time in my life, I at least had the vision of becoming an independent artist, the passion and driving force needed to do so.

Salma Hayek fueled my heart even more. Besides Christina Ricci, she was one of my movie star crushes as a young, 24/7 hard-on teenage boy. I dreamt of her scene from Dusk til Dawn, from dusk til dawn and Desperado was one of those films that I watched over, and over, and over again. It had it all, a hot woman, with exotic sex appeal, a teenage boy fantasizes about, and it was a bad ass film. And also I admit it I wanted to be Antonio Banderas, he was this suave bad ass, who fought off a gang of drug runners, sang and played the guitar, and got Salma Hayek. Everything a teenage boy dreams to be all in one package, a badass, a rock star, and getting the hot girl; thank you Robert Rodriguez. Without you neither Desperado or from Dusk til Dawn would have existed. And I wouldn't have discovered Quentin Tarantino.

I watched Desperado and From Dusk Til Dawn before ever seeing Pulp Fiction. Quentin Tarantino's bar scene in Desperado, him getting shot in the fucking face, and the estranged psychotic character he played, Richard Gecko, in From Dusk Til Dawn, was all I needed to give me the curiosity to find more films he was in and wrote. I admit it, I only watched Pulp Fiction a handful of times, from middle school until I started college. And it would be my freshman year in college when I would watch Pulp Fiction, with a deeper analysis, and see Reservoir Dogs, and True Romance for the first time. Not only that but I would learn more about and watch more Stanley Kubrick films as well. Thank you MD, my freshman year dorm room neighbor, sophomore year roommate, and Stockton soccer teammate, you introduced me to more serious films. Many days and nights were spent in the P-dorms, watching films such as Apocalypse Now, A Clockwork Orange, The Big Lewbowski, Goodfellas, The Godfather trilogy, many, many others, and of course, True Romance. This was my film school; my roommates and neighbors, and I spent many hours watching, drinking, discussing, critiquing, and quoting from the many films we watched. And also during this time, it was the birth of DVD. I little by little built my library of DVDs, and one of the wonders of DVD, were the extras which came with each film. DVDs were now a tool used to learn about the film making process. And Tarantino and Rodriguez offered a lot with their behind the scenes film making process. This was my film school and amongst others they were my film professors.

Tarantino's writing and filming process and Rodriguez's 5 minutes film school segments have been very informative and inspiring as well. They modeled the type of independent artist and writer I wanted to be. And finally when I began to watch and focus on Stanley Kubrick's films, his life, and his film making process, I developed the awareness and scope of what it takes to not only be a successful independent artist but a genuine one as well.

Stanley Kubrick's eccentricity and perfectionism were two things I could relate to. Many late nights drinking and watching his films, such as 2001: A Space Odyssey, Eyes Wide Shut, A Clockwork Orange, and The Shining, alone and creating this isolation within the average joe, 9 to 5 world I was a part of was crucial, it was necessary, and turned me into a daring, free spirited artist, yet, a stranger slowly descending into deeper waters in the eyes of those close to me who didn't understand the new me, or the real me, fighting, pulling, tearing his way out of this phantom self, the false identity I've been living for most of my life. It was liberating, and also an awakening process, which I slowly, slowly, began to experience. And in Stanley Kubrick and his work I not only discovered an articulate, yet, bold way of writing for someone of his time, but deeper meanings hidden within his work; The Da Vinci Code was big at this time, but I was little, by little discovering The Kubrick Code. With Kubrick I realized that you can create bold, serious stories, yet, intertwine it together with witty and funny dialogue, and weave in between the lines hidden messages. Call it conspiracy, call it delusional, whatever, it's there; others have researched and discovered for themselves Kubrick's hidden messages about the Apollo 11 Moon Landing, Mind Control, and Secret Societies. Kubrick had not only great vision as a photographer/filmmaker, but was able to write and tell a story in a way, that his characters, plots, dialogue, and images are forever implanted in the human mind, and psyche.

For me Kubrick was like Leonardo Da Vinci, he created a handful of master pieces with discipline, a hard strict work ethic (which could be considered insane, but aren't all brilliant minds given such negative titles), and an abstract approach in the way he creates. Trent Reznor, on his own created beautiful, yet, dreary music which could be uplifting and transcending, Robert Rodriguez, was a one man force who did it all, wrote, directed, produced and played the music for his films; as an artist he was his own maestro, and Quentin Tarantino who also wrote and directed his own films, as a writer is able to give his characters a real, free flowing voice with his quick, edgy dialogue.

My 4 years living at the Richard Stockton College of New Jersey, and the 2 years I spent living like a vagabond, commuting 2 days a week to finish school, was a major transit period in my life. I was transforming from athlete to artist. I bulked up on art classes, and ended up graduating with an arts degree in art history. Without Kubrick, Reznor, Rodriguez, and Tarantino I wouldn't have the inspiration or the modeling to write the way I write. Films were more influential with my writing, not novels. I write, and I am a story teller. For now I write books, soon spend more time writing screenplays, and sometime further down the road I will make films. But, not yet, there are still more books and stories for me to tell on paper first.

Social Media, Films and the binge watching generation

Why would anyone want to read a book, when you have the crack, cocaine, crystal meth, and heroine, which is Netflix, the internet, social media, and television at your fingertips? Esperanza was written in an unconventional, nonlinear manner due to my love of film, and the couple of T.V. series which influenced me as a writer (The Sopranos, and Lost); with the Sopranos being a dramedy, having comedy weaved into a dark, dramatic storyline, and Lost, using flashbacks and flash-forwards, as a way to tell a story. It's evident that I have no literature background or influences, and do not write and follow the literary rules of how a book is written, based on narrative, structure, size, and word count. Yes, there are rules for how long a novel, or a screenplay should be written, and how long a film or an episode should be, and how all should be made and told, but rules throughout time have always been made to be broken.

I know that as an indie author I should be preaching about reading books and the 100 plus books I read every year, but that's not me. I'm a product of this instant entertainment gratification generation, and admit that I'm not an avid reader. I'm a storyteller who reads to learn. Books of fiction aren't books I prefer to read; instead I enjoy reading books about history, different cultures, the esoteric, supernatural, new age, biographies, autobiographies, and books written by influential investigative journalists and whistleblowers. I crave reading books with information, not entertainment. For entertainment I love movies. So, the combination of books I love to read and the movies I love to watch helped influence and mold the writing style that I have. Will this change and evolve over time absolutely.

The art of storytelling

From sitting around a fire, to sitting before a stage, to sitting near a radio, to sitting before a television, to sitting with a hand size phone screen held in your palm, no matter how vast the platform for telling a story has changed, the art of storytelling will never die. Story telling is woven within our DNA; it's a part of who we are as human beings. That's what we do all day, every day, is tell or show stories. We bullshit at the watercooler, in the checkout line, we vent, and tell each other about our awesome day, shitty day, or the hot chick at the gym. We always want to know about what happened the night before, over the weekend, or how was the date with so and so. "You won't fucking believe what just happened. . . " or "Guess what?" Yeah these are some typical open lines we hear all the time, and no matter how many times we use them, they never get old or die. So, as a story teller we have to find new and inventive ways to tell our stories. Therefore, how can there be rules. In a world of so many there are billions of stories that have been told or are waiting to be told; and that's just from life experiences, add in stories created from our imaginations, and manifested in our minds, the stories to be told are infinite. So, who's to say what stories work or do not? Who's to say what is marketable or not? Who's to say what is politically correct or not? Who to say if it's worth telling or not?

So do not be afraid to tell your story. If you have an idea in your mind, water it every day until it grows into a completed manuscript, and then blossoms into a published book. Write without fear of what is right or wrong, or politically correct. Write what's in your heart, be authentic and never hold back. No matter who you are, you are a storyteller and have within you the ability to write a book.

Writer-Author-Artist

From the very beginning I wasn't sure what my title should be or how I should be recognized. Am I a writer? Am I an author? Am I an artist? Being where I am now, I'd say that I am all three. Obviously a writer writes, so does an author, but an author ends up being someone who has written, usually something from nothing. This seems to be the basic difference; that an author usually uses their imagination and creates characters and a world, and a writer is someone either in the early stages of creating, yet, also writes blogs, essays, poems, news articles, advertisements, etc.. As for an artist, well, an artist seems to be the umbrella for being a writer and an author, since an artist creates. Therefore, I see myself as a writer, as an author, and as an artist; I am an independent artist/author.

From Idea to Print

From Aspiring Writer to Indie Author

Every story begins with a thought, an idea. After the seed is planted, it little by little grows, and then evolves like a child with lots of nurturing and care. The writing process and the journey I began in 2007 has been not only exciting, but at times a burden, yet in the end rewarding. No matter how many drafts I've written, how many notebooks I've filled, napkins and scraps of paper I've written on, how many times the story has changed, or characters being added or taken away, how stressful it's been or how many times I wanted to give up, stop, or kill myself, I wouldn't change a damn thing about the ten year journey I took with Esperanza.

For aspiring writers I encourage you to take that first step. If you have an idea or a story in you get it out, write that first word. Even if you don't have a clue how to begin or where to go know that if you devote yourself and you are passionate about what you write, it can be done. No matter where the road takes you, as long as you have the will power to carry on when the writing becomes difficult, it seems to never end or leading to nowhere, when roadblocks and failed attempts occur, believe in yourself and your work, and when you get to the end you'll have your book.

Trust in the process, no matter what that may be for you. It's the process and how you execute that will pave the way. Be sure to map out every possible road and have the vision to foresee what lies ahead. The basic character traits, that of a warrior, an entrepreneur, and a curious scholar are just some of the human qualities that most writers must possess. Just being an intellectual or a dreamer is like going out to sea without a sail or oars. Have balance within you and your life. Find a way to make it work and be able to adapt to any changes or barriers. The writing process is grueling yet rewarding. Know this though, no matter who you are, it can be done. Believe in you and your idea. Trust in and follow your heart and it will take you there.

About

    Tommy Tutalo is an independent author, writer, photographer, painter, and visual artist, whose work is considered to be diverse, and universal. A native of West Orange, New Jersey, Tommy comes from a hardworking, and loving blue-collar background, and grew up in an ethnically diverse community. Both Tommy's up-bringing, and the melting pot he grew up in have been two influential factors in his life and the arts. At an early age Tommy discovered a love for both the arts and the beautiful game, soccer. Soccer would become Tommy's outlet and craft, which he would nourish and pursue, putting the arts off as secondary. Tommy's hard work ethic, devotion, and perseverance with soccer, would enable Tommy to play at a very high level during his adolescent years, becoming one of the most decorated and recognized players in New Jersey, and eventually sought by, and play for The Richard Stockton College of New Jersey, where he would win a DIV. III National Championship with the 2001 team. This would be the pinnacle of Tommy's soccer career, and the foundation for the next phase in his life. As one door shut, another door opened, and Tommy would then pursue the arts, learning many different art mediums during, and after graduating from college, with a Bachelor of the Arts degree, Art History, and by any means devote his life to living as an independent artist and author.

After the release of Tommy's debut novel Esperanza, which acquired rave reviews ". . .heart-wrenchingly good . . ." ". . .epic in scale . . ." "An often enthralling tale of how a strong family can withstand anything." "The setting is cunningly done and the characters leap off the pages with a lot of life." it has been taking on a life of its own. Esperanza is a story which revolves around the illegal immigration situation at the U.S. Mexico border. A reflection of the current times, Esperanza focuses on the darker side of illegal immigration and how a modest dreamer can get caught up in a life of crime in order to cross over the border and survive in the United States while seeking to live the American Dream.

Tommy is currently working on his second novel, The Mime a fantasy tale about how a young girl helps a mime retrieve his voice which was stolen from a magical villain seeking vengeance.

Body of Work

Esperanza

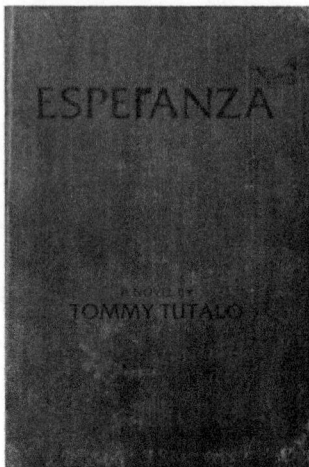

Three journals left behind by Gabriela, after her untimely death, for her daughter, Sarita, a young adult, become windows into the past. The past then becomes alive, as Sarita reads through the journals, and learns more about the life of Gabriela, an illegal immigrant from Mexico, who seeks the American Dream, and Dante, an artist, who seeks redemption. Both are united and divided by a crime syndicate, Nada Mas, and eventually, what binds them back together is a child, Sarita. It is after both Gabriela and Dante break ties with Nada Mas that Gabriela is abducted, held captive, and forcefully deported back to Mexico, and Dante, who is seeking refuge in Mexico, takes Sarita with him, from New Jersey, cross country, to Mexico, and back, all while two separate branches of the FBI

As an indie author all the support is greatly appreciated. Please consider leaving a review on Amazon for this book, Esperanza, and my other books.

Social Media

E-Mail- tommytutalo@gmail.com

Website- www.tommytutalo.com

Linkedin- https://www.linkedin.com/in/tommy-tutalo-a3329a32/

Facebook- https://www.facebook.com/TommyTutalo.Author/

Instagram- https://www.instagram.com/tommytutalo/

Special Thanks

Thank you Joey Tutalo, a graphic designer who created the cover art and photography for the books Esperanza and An Indie Author's way. For any queries please contact Joey Tutalo at Jtutalo@me.com

www.ingramcontent.com/pod-product-compliance
Lightning Source LLC
Chambersburg PA
CBHW051727040426
42447CB00008B/1004